ECONOMIC ISSUES, PROBLEMS AND PERSPECTIVES

# IMPROPER PAYMENTS AND RECOVERY AUDITS OF FEDERAL AGENCIES

# LEGISLATION AND ANALYSES

# ECONOMIC ISSUES, PROBLEMS AND PERSPECTIVES

Additional books in this series can be found on Nova's website under the Series tab.

Additional e-books in this series can be found on Nova's website under the e-book tab.

ECONOMIC ISSUES, PROBLEMS AND PERSPECTIVES

# IMPROPER PAYMENTS AND RECOVERY AUDITS OF FEDERAL AGENCIES

## LEGISLATION AND ANALYSES

JEFFREY B. POWERS
EDITOR

NOVINKA

*New York*

**Library of Congress Cataloging-in-Publication Data**

ISBN: 978-1-62948-844-8

*Published by Nova Science Publishers, Inc. † New York*

# CONTENTS

# PREFACE

As Congress searches for ways to generate savings, reduce the deficit, and fund federal programs, it has held hearings and passed legislation to prevent and recover improper payments. Improper payments are payments made in an incorrect amount, payments that should not have been made at all, or payments made to an ineligible recipient or for an ineligible purpose. The total amount of improper payments may be even higher than reported because several agencies have yet to determine improper payment amounts for many programs, including some with billions of dollars in annual expenditures. This book discusses the legislation, implementation and analysis of improper payments and recovery audits. The authors of this book also provide a testimony on the remaining challenges and strategies for governmentwide reduction efforts of improper payments, and a testimony on new steps to strengthen the integrity of federal payments.

Chapter 1 - As Congress searches for ways to generate savings, reduce the deficit, and fund federal programs, it has held hearings and passed legislation to prevent and recover improper payments. Improper payments—which exceeded $115 billion in FY2011—are payments made in an incorrect amount, payments that should not have been made at all, or payments made to an ineligible recipient or for an ineligible purpose. The total amount of improper payments may be even higher than reported because several agencies have yet to determine improper payment amounts for many programs, including some with billions of dollars in annual expenditures.

In 2002, Congress passed the Improper Payments Information Act (IPIA; P.L. 107-300; 116 Stat. 2350), which established an initial framework for identifying, measuring, preventing, and reporting on improper payments at each agency. That same year, Congress also passed legislation, the Recovery

Audit Act (P.L. 107-107; Section 831; 115 Stat. 1186), which required agencies that awarded more than $500 million annually in contracts to establish programs to recover overpayments to contractors.

After five years of reporting, the data indicated that while many individual programs reduced their improper payment rates, the total amount of improper payments and the government-wide improper payment rate both increased. Since the IPIA reporting requirements took effect, agencies have expanded the number of programs reported each year. One potential consequence of this expansion is that the annual dollar amount of improper payments reported has more than doubled over time from $45 billion in FY2004 to $108 billion in FY2012.

In response, Congress passed new legislation, the Improper Payments Elimination and Recovery Act of 2010 (IPERA, P.L. 111-204; 124 Stat. 2224), which replaced and consolidated the requirements of both IPIA and the Recovery Audit Act. IPERA retained the core provisions of the IPIA while requiring improvements in agency improper payment estimation methodologies and improper payment reduction plans. It also significantly expanded the scope and reporting requirements of recovery audit programs.

A subsequent statute, the Improper Payments Elimination and Recovery Improvement Act of 2012 (IPERIA; P.L. 112-248), signed into law on January 10, 2013, addresses some of the weaknesses in agency improper payment prevention controls and recovery audit programs. In particular, IPERIA requires agencies to improve the quality of oversight for high-dollar and high-risk programs, and it mandates that agencies share data regarding recipient eligibility and payment amounts. In addition, IPERIA requires the Office of Management and Budget to examine the rates and amounts of improper payments that agencies have recovered and establish targets for increasing those amounts.

Chapter 2 - Over the past decade, GAO has issued numerous reports and testimonies highlighting improper payment issues across the federal government as well as at specific agencies. Fiscal year 2011 marked the eighth year of implementation of the Improper Payments Information Act of 2002 (IPIA), as well as the first year of implementation for the Improper Payments Elimination and Recovery Act of 2010 (IPERA). IPIA requires executive branch agencies to annually identify programs and activities susceptible to significant improper payments, estimate the amount of improper payments for such programs and activities, and report these estimates along with actions taken to reduce them. IPERA amended IPIA and expanded requirements for recovering overpayments across a broad range of federal programs.

This testimony addresses (1) federal agencies' reported progress in estimating and reducing improper payments; (2) challenges in meeting current requirements to estimate and evaluate improper payments, including the results of GAO's case study of the estimation methodology and corrective actions for the Foster Care program; and (3) possible strategies that can be taken to move forward in reducing improper payments. This testimony is primarily based on prior GAO reports, including the report released today on improper payment estimates in the Foster Care program. It also includes unaudited improper payment information recently presented in federal entities' fiscal year 2011 performance and accountability reports and agency financial reports.

Chapter 3 – This chapter is testimony of Daniel I. Werfel, Controller, Office of Management and Budget at a hearing on "Curbing Federal Agency Waste and Fraud: New Steps to Strengthen the Integrity of Federal Payment".

In: Improper Payments ...
Editor: Jeffrey B. Powers

ISBN: 978-1-62948-844-8


*Chapter 1*

# IMPROPER PAYMENTS AND RECOVERY AUDITS: LEGISLATION, IMPLEMENTATION, AND ANALYSIS*

*Garrett Hatch*

## SUMMARY

As Congress searches for ways to generate savings, reduce the deficit, and fund federal programs, it has held hearings and passed legislation to prevent and recover improper payments. Improper payments—which exceeded $115 billion in FY2011—are payments made in an incorrect amount, payments that should not have been made at all, or payments made to an ineligible recipient or for an ineligible purpose. The total amount of improper payments may be even higher than reported because several agencies have yet to determine improper payment amounts for many programs, including some with billions of dollars in annual expenditures.

In 2002, Congress passed the Improper Payments Information Act (IPIA; P.L. 107-300; 116 Stat. 2350), which established an initial framework for identifying, measuring, preventing, and reporting on improper payments at each agency. That same year, Congress also passed legislation, the Recovery Audit Act (P.L. 107-107; Section 831; 115 Stat. 1186), which required

* This is an edited, reformatted and augmented version of a Congressional Research Service publication, CRS Report for Congress R42878, dated October 18, 2013.

agencies that awarded more than $500 million annually in contracts to establish programs to recover overpayments to contractors.

After five years of reporting, the data indicated that while many individual programs reduced their improper payment rates, the total amount of improper payments and the government-wide improper payment rate both increased. Since the IPIA reporting requirements took effect, agencies have expanded the number of programs reported each year. One potential consequence of this expansion is that the annual dollar amount of improper payments reported has more than doubled over time from $45 billion in FY2004 to $108 billion in FY2012.

In response, Congress passed new legislation, the Improper Payments Elimination and Recovery Act of 2010 (IPERA, P.L. 111-204; 124 Stat. 2224), which replaced and consolidated the requirements of both IPIA and the Recovery Audit Act. IPERA retained the core provisions of the IPIA while requiring improvements in agency improper payment estimation methodologies and improper payment reduction plans. It also significantly expanded the scope and reporting requirements of recovery audit programs.

A subsequent statute, the Improper Payments Elimination and Recovery Improvement Act of 2012 (IPERIA; P.L. 112-248), signed into law on January 10, 2013, addresses some of the weaknesses in agency improper payment prevention controls and recovery audit programs. In particular, IPERIA requires agencies to improve the quality of oversight for high-dollar and high-risk programs, and it mandates that agencies share data regarding recipient eligibility and payment amounts. In addition, IPERIA requires the Office of Management and Budget to examine the rates and amounts of improper payments that agencies have recovered and establish targets for increasing those amounts.

# IMPROPER PAYMENTS ELIMINATION AND RECOVERY ACT OF 2010

## Background

In an effort to reduce and ultimately eliminate billions of dollars in improper payments made by federal agencies each fiscal year, Congress passed the Improper Payments Information Act (IPIA; P.L. 107-300; 116 Stat. 2350) in 2002. IPIA established an initial framework for identifying, measuring, preventing, and reporting on improper payments at each agency. Separately, Congress also passed legislation, the Recovery Audit Act of 2002 (P.L. 107-107; Section 831; 115 Stat. 1186), which required agencies that awarded more than $500 million annually in contracts to implement plans to recover overpayments to contractors.[1]

Reports on improper payments and recovery audits were first issued for FY2004. After five years of reporting, the data showed that progress under IPIA was uneven—while many individual programs reduced their improper payment rates, the total amount of improper payments and the government-wide improper payment rate both increased between FY2004 and FY2008. During that same time period, Government Accountability Office (GAO) auditors had identified weaknesses in numerous agencies' recovery audit programs.[2]

In response, Congress passed new legislation, the Improper Payments Elimination and Recovery Act of 2010 (IPERA; P.L. 111-204; 124 Stat. 2224), which replaced and consolidated the requirements of both IPIA and the Recovery Audit Act. As discussed below, IPERA retained the core provisions of the IPIA while requiring improvements in agency improper payment estimation methodologies and improper payment reduction plans. It also significantly expanded the scope and reporting requirements of recovery audit programs.

## Improper Payments

IPERA defines an improper payment as a payment that should not have been made or that was made in an incorrect amount, including both overpayments and underpayments. This definition includes payments that were made to an ineligible recipient, duplicate payments, payments for a good or service not received, and payments that do not account for credit for applicable discounts. Under IPERA, "payment" is defined as a transfer or commitment to transfer federal funds in the future—including cash, securities, loans, loan guarantees, and insurance subsidies—to a nonfederal entity. Thus, the law applies to federal funds paid or obligated by a federal agency to nonfederal grantees, contractors, and loan recipients, including state or local governments who administer federal programs or activities.

***Risk Assessments***

IPERA requires agencies to take specific steps to identify and reduce improper payments. First, it requires agencies to perform a risk assessment of all programs and activities and identify those that were susceptible to "significant" improper payments. IPERA defines "significant" for FY2011 and FY2012 as either (1) improper payments that exceed both $10 million and 2.5% of program or activity outlays; or (2) improper payments in excess of $100 million. Beginning in FY2013, the 2.5% threshold drops to 1.5%, with other aspects of the definition unchanged. IPERA also requires agencies to perform the initial risk assessment for every program and activity during the year in which IPERA was enacted (i.e., in 2011) and to perform subsequent risk assessments at least every three years.

When performing risk assessments, IPERA requires agencies to consider several risk factors that may make a program or activity susceptible to "significant" improper payments:

- whether the program or activity is new to the agency;
- the complexity of the program or activity;
- the volume of payments;
- whether payments or payment eligibility decisions are made outside the agency, such as by a state government;
- recent major changes in program funding, authorities, practices, or procedures;
- the level of experience and quality of training for personnel responsible for making program eligibility determinations or certifying that payments are accurate; and
- major deficiencies in an agency's audit report or other source that might result in inaccurate payment certification.

Once a program or activity has been identified as susceptible to "significant" improper payments, agencies are required to estimate the amount of improper payments made under each.

***Reporting on Agency Efforts to Reduce Improper Payments***

IPERA requires agencies to report on the actions they have taken to reduce improper payments for each program and activity in the accompanying materials to their annual financial statement. IPERA also requires agencies to provide an estimate of improper payments for each program or activity identified as susceptible through the risk assessment, describe the causes of improper payments, the actions planned or taken to correct those problems, and when those actions were completed or will be completed. Target dates for achieving reductions in improper payments must be approved by the Office of Management and Budget (OMB), and agencies must include annual performance criteria used to hold the appropriate parties accountable for meeting those targets— whether they work for the agency or for a state or local government that helps implement the program. The performance criteria must also include an evaluation of the internal controls within the agency, or state or local government, that are intended to prevent, detect, and recover improper payments. IPERA also requires agencies to include a statement as to whether they have sufficient resources to develop their own internal controls for reducing improper payments—such as human capital and information systems—and, if not, to identify what additional resources are needed to do so. OMB is also required to establish criteria that agencies must meet to demonstrate that they have effective internal control systems.

IPERA also requires OMB to submit a report to two congressional committees—the House Committee on Oversight and Government Reform and the Senate Committee on Homeland Security and Government Affairs—that provides a government-wide summary of agency efforts to reduce and recover improper payments. This report must include (1) government-wide improper payment reduction targets; (2) the compliance status of each agency; (3) a discussion of progress made towards meeting improper payment reduction targets; and (4) a summary of the improper payment reduction and recovery actions of each agency. IPERA further directs OMB to provide guidance on the timing and format of the improper payments reports required by IPERA, both at the agency level and government wide. OMB's guidance, which was issued in 2011, is discussed in detail in the "OMB Guidance" section of this chapter.

### *Compliance*

The inspector general of each agency must determine whether the agency is in compliance with IPERA and report its findings to the head of the agency, the Comptroller General, the House Committee on Oversight and Government Reform, and the Senate Committee on Homeland Security and Government Affairs. An agency is deemed in compliance if it has

- published an annual financial statement;
- conducted risk assessments for each program or activity;

- published improper payment estimates, corrective action plans, and improper payment reduction targets for all risk-susceptible programs and activities; and
- reported no improper payment rate that met or exceeded 10%.

By definition, then, an agency must report that all of its programs and activities have an improper payment rate of less than 10% to be deemed in compliance with IPERA.

Agencies that are deemed noncompliant must submit a plan to Congress that describes the steps they will take to become fully compliant. The plan must include (1) measurable milestones that will result in compliance for each program or activity deemed noncompliant; (2) the name of a senior agency official who is responsible for ensuring the agency becomes compliant; and (3) an "accountability mechanism" that may include incentives and consequences tied to the ability of the responsible official to bring the agency into compliance.

If an agency is deemed noncompliant for two consecutive years, and OMB has determined that additional funding would help the agency become compliant, then the agency head would be required to obligate additional funds—in an amount determined by OMB—for "intensified compliance efforts." IPERA does not provide agencies with new authority for transferring funds. Agencies that were unable to obligate all of the additional funds required by OMB under their existing authorities, then, would need statutory authority to transfer funds under Title 31 of the *U.S. Code*.[3]

If an agency is deemed noncompliant for three or more consecutive years for the same program or activity, then the agency must submit to Congress reauthorization proposals for those programs or activities, along with proposed statutory changes that may bring the agency into compliance.

IPERA gives OMB the authority to conduct compliance pilot programs to "test potential accountability mechanisms" and to report the findings from those pilot programs within five years from enactment (i.e., before July 22, 2015).

## Recovery Audits

A recovery audit, or payment recapture audit, is a review process designed to identify overpayments. According to OMB guidance,[4] "It is not an audit in the traditional sense. Rather it is a detective and corrective control activity designed to identify and recapture overpayments, and, as such, is a management function and responsibility."[5]

The idea of recouping overpayments through the recovery auditing process had received attention in previous Congresses. In a hearing on eliminating agency payment errors, Senator Tom Carper[6] noted that, "even as agencies report greater improper payments, we are seeing actually fewer improper payments recovered."[7] When Senator Carper introduced IPERA in the 110th Congress, the legislation addressed this issue through the inclusion of a section on recovery audits.

IPERA requires agencies to perform recovery audits on each program or activity[8] with expenditures of $1 million or more per year. In addition, the legislation stipulates that the performance of recovery audits is conditional on cost-effectiveness, though the term "cost- effective" is not defined in law. IPERA contains provisions for the conduct of these recovery audits.[9] The legislation establishes agencies' threshold requirement for recovery auditing, details certain procedures for the performance of recovery audits, mandates collection of overpayments, specifies disposition allotments for recovered amounts, and imposes reporting requirements on actions to recover improper payments.

The legislation institutes two procedural requirements for the conduct of recovery audits. First, it requires agencies to prioritize both the most recent payments and those deemed susceptible to "significant" improper payments. Second, the legislation specifies options for recovery audit services—they could be performed within the agency itself or by other U.S. departments and agencies, or private sector services could be procured by contract.

Although IPERA permits contractors to conduct recovery audits on agencies' behalf, it circumscribes their scope of authority. Only with the express consent of the agency head are contractors authorized to notify entities of potential overpayments,[10] respond to questions pertaining to potential overpayments, and take administrative action on overpayment claims. In addition, contractors are not allowed to render a final decision as to whether or not an overpayment occurred, and they are not authorized to adjudicate overpayment claims. IPERA requires recovery audit contractors to report all overpayments detected through recovery audits to the procuring agency, regardless of whether a given overpayment occurred at the agency that contracted the audit or another agency beyond the scope of the contract.

Nongovernmental entities are prohibited from disclosing information uncovered through a recovery audit that would identify an individual for any purpose other than the recovery audit itself. An individual could waive this privacy protection, however, and permit the executive agency that contracted the audit to disclose identifying information for other purposes.

The legislation directs agencies to take "prompt and appropriate action" to collect overpayments identified in recovery audits upon receipt of an overpayment notification. Distribution of collected amounts was left to the discretion of agency heads, though there were limits on the maximum percentage of recovered amounts that could be applied to certain programs, purposes, and activities:

- At most, 25% for a financial management improvement program, to be implemented by agency heads to address improper payments and reduce errors and waste across agency programs and operations.
- At most, 25% credited to the appropriation or fund from which the overpayment was made.
- At most, 5% for inspector general activities relating to implementation of the legislation itself or investigation of improper payments.
- The remaining 45% of collected amounts—and up to 100% depending on how much the agencies actually allocated in accordance with these criteria—are to be deposited in the Treasury as miscellaneous receipts.

IPERA specifies four reporting requirements which relate to the conduct of recovery audits. First, the legislation requires agency heads to provide a report on improper payment recovery actions, which is to include a statistically valid estimate of improper payments made by each program or activity, along with the following:

- a discussion of the methods used to recover overpayments;
- the amounts recovered, outstanding, and determined not to be collectable;
- a written justification explaining any uncollected amounts;
- an aging schedule of outstanding amounts;[11]
- a summary of the disposition of recovered amounts;
- a discussion of conditions giving rise to improper payments and how these are being resolved; and
- if an agency determined that a recovery audit was not cost-effective, then a justification as to why.[12]

Second, by November 1 of each year, agencies are required to submit a report to OMB and Congress on actions taken on those conditions that promote overpayments, as identified and reported by recovery audit contractors. Third, the Director of OMB must provide the Senate Committee on Homeland Security and Governmental Affairs and the House Committee on Oversight and Government Reform a government-wide report on agencies' reports of improper payments information and recovery actions, as well as the compliance status of each agency covered by the law. Lastly, within two years of IPERA's enactment, the Chief Financial Officers Council must conduct a study, in consultation with the Council of Inspectors General on Integrity and Efficiency and recovery audit experts, on the implementation of IPERA's recovery audit provisions, the costs and benefits of agency recovery audit activities, and, in particular, the effectiveness of service provision by private contractors, agency employees, cross-servicing from other agencies, or any combination of the three. A report on this study was to be submitted to the Senate Committee on Homeland Security and Governmental Affairs, the House Committee on Oversight and Government Reform, and the Comptroller General by July 22, 2012.[13]

## OMB GUIDANCE

OMB circulars operationalize implementation for agencies. Frequently, if legislation gives OMB discretion over administrative concerns, OMB details the legislation's procedural requirements and may impose its own additional requirements, provided that these do not contravene the enacted legislation. IPERA requires OMB to issue implementation guidance to agencies. This government-wide guidance was issued April 11, 2011, through the revision of Appendix C of OMB Circular A-123 (hereinafter, A-123), *Management's Responsibility for Internal Control.*[14] Agencies were required to begin using the revised guidance for their FY2011 reporting.

### Improper Payments

OMB's definition of an improper payment is consistent with IPERA's, though A-123 clarifies that when an agency does not have the documentation necessary to determine that a payment was proper, it is to be considered improper. OMB's guidance also provides a definition for program, which IPERA does not.[15] According to A-123, a program includes all types of grants, procurements, and credit programs, as well as regulatory activities, research and development activities, and activities that agencies perform to support their programs. OMB's guidance specifies that payments to other agencies and to employees are not considered programs.

***Risk Assessments***

A-123, like IPERA, requires agencies to (1) review all programs and identify those susceptible to improper payments; (2) develop a valid estimate of the amount of improper payments for those programs identified as susceptible to "significant" improper payments; (3) implement a plan to reduce improper payments; and (4) report estimates of the annual amounts of improper payments and progress in reducing them. For each of those steps, discussed below, A-123 establishes a detailed process by which agencies are to fulfill their obligations under IPERA.

A-123 and IPERA both use the same definition of "significant" improper payments for agencies to follow when identifying programs susceptible to improper payments, including the use of a 2.5% threshold for FY2011 and FY2012, and a 1.5% threshold for FY2013 and beyond. The guidance and IPERA also identified the same risk factors that may indicate a program is susceptible to "significant" improper payments. OMB may determine on a case-by-case basis whether certain programs below the threshold may be required to have risk assessments performed.

Like IPERA, A-123 requires OMB to approve of agency sampling methodologies to ensure they accurately reflect the annual amount of improper payments. A-123 provides agencies with detailed explanations of steps they should take to establish valid methodologies, including sampling technique and size. OMB's guidance specifies that improper payment estimates should only include the erroneous amount. For example, if a payment of $50 was due, and the agency paid $60, then only the $10 above the correct amount would be counted in the improper payment total. Similarly, if the agency had paid $40 to a recipient that was supposed to receive $50, then only the $10 below the correct amount would be counted as improper. However, if a $100 payment was made without sufficient documentation to confirm that the payment was correct, the entire $100 would be included in the improper payment total. A-123 permits agencies to sample transactions at certain steps within the lifecycle of a payment rather than the entire payment process, if the agency believes that only those steps have the highest risk or have the greatest return on investment. For example, if an agency determines that a five-step payment has two high-risk steps, then it may sample, review, and report an estimate for just those two steps.

A-123 mirrors IPERA in that it requires each agency to develop a plan to reduce improper payments that includes three components: a description of the root causes of improper payments for each risk-susceptible program; OMB-approved improper payment reduction targets and a timeline within which those targets will be reached; and the steps taken to ensure that all of the parties involved—federal and nonfederal—are held accountable. The guidance does not provide examples of accountability mechanisms, but it does require agencies to assess whether they or their partners have the necessary infrastructure (i.e., human capital, internal controls, information systems) to reduce improper payments. A-123, like IPERA, also requires agencies to identify any statutory or regulatory barriers to implementing their plans. However, A-123 permits agencies to request a waiver for this reporting for programs or activities that have been deemed not risk- susceptible for two consecutive years, an allowance which is not found in IPERA.

A-123 requires agencies to include an estimate of the annual amount of improper payments for all of their programs and activities, and it clarifies that the estimate is to include programs or activities with estimated improper payment totals below $10 million. Consistent with IPERA, OMB's guidance also requires agencies to publish a report each year that includes the improper payment estimate; narrative information on agency plans to prevent, detect, and recover improper payments; and what resources, if any, they lack to implement their plans.

### *Compliance*

A-123 provides numerous examples of steps agencies should take to prevent, detect, and recapture improper payments. The guidance acknowledges that fully implementing long-term corrective actions may take several years, but that those actions should be intensified and expanded whenever possible. A-123 identifies best-practices that could be used by agencies to reduce and recover improper payments, including predictive modeling, forensic accounting, partnering with agency inspectors general to focus on fraud prevention, data mining, and training agency staff on tools to identify improper payments.

## Recovery Audits

As noted, IPERA requires agencies that have programs or activities with expenditures of $1 million or more per fiscal year to conduct payment recapture audits. A-123 further requires agencies to implement payment recapture audit programs, which consist of overall plans for risk analysis, payment recapture audits, and recapture (recovery) activities.[16] While the agency head has discretion over the manner and combination of payment recapture activities, the cost- effectiveness mandate means that the benefits of the payment recapture audit program, such as recaptured amounts, should exceed the costs of implementation and oversight. Payment recapture activities should include a management improvement program to address problems with internal controls that contributed to those overpayments identified through implementation of a payment recapture program.

A-123's scope for payment recapture audit programs is consistent with IPERA, though A-123 provides greater specificity regarding the types of programs and activities which require recovery audits, including grants, benefits, loans, and contract programs. In addition, A-123 states that agencies

- must prioritize payment recapture audits for the most recent payments and those deemed susceptible to "significant" improper payments;
- must design the program so as to ensure the greatest financial benefit for the government;
- may exclude payments from recovery audit activities if payment recapture audits are not determined to be cost-effective;
- may permit payment recapture audit contractors to notify entities of potential overpayments, respond to questions about overpayments, and take administrative action on overpayment claims but cannot authorize these contractors to render a final decision as to whether or not an overpayment occurred nor to adjudicate overpayment claims; and
- must correct underpayments identified through the recovery audit process, as well as overpayments.[17]

IPERA requires agencies to perform recovery audits if doing so is cost-effective. According to A-123, agencies should consider the likelihood of overpayment recapture in determining whether a recapture audit is cost-effective. In making this determination, agencies may weigh (1) whether laws or regulations permit recovery; (2) whether the recipient of the overpayment is likely to have resources to repay overpayments from nonfederal funds; (3) whether the evidence of overpayment is clear versus contestable; and (4) whether the overpayment is truly a recoverable improper payment rather than a payment with unsupported documentation.[18]

If an agency determines that a payment recapture audit program would not be cost-effective, then it must advise OMB and the agency's inspector general of this decision, along with the analysis it performed to reach that decision. OMB may review the analysis and instruct the agency to conduct a payment recapture audit program.

Agencies are required to establish annual payment recapture targets for their programs, which should vary in accordance with the different types of payments the agency makes, such as grants versus contracts. Targets are based on the rate of recovery, which the guidance defines as "the amount of improper payments recovered divided by the amount of improper payments identified." Agencies may set their own targets for OMB review and approval but must aim for annual recapture targets of at least 85% within three years.[19] If they cannot achieve this target by FY2013, they must provide OMB a justification for setting a lowered target and obtain OMB's approval before setting it.

A-123 establishes guidelines for coordination between federal agencies and state or local governments, with respect to both payment recapture audits and financial management improvement efforts authorized by IPERA. Grant programs are subject to IPERA's recovery audit provisions, as noted previously, and these programs are often administered by states and local governments. The guidance instructs federal agencies to work with state and local governments to ensure that sufficient resources are available to perform payment recapture audits; federal agencies must also coordinate among themselves to reach partnerships with grant recipients for cost-effective payment recapture audit implementation. In addition, agency heads are required to use information obtained from payment recapture programs to implement financial management improvement programs that will improve the agency's internal controls to address improper payments, as well as reduce errors and waste across agency programs and operations. In so doing, agencies with state-administered programs may provide money to states and local governments for their financial management improvement efforts.[20]

IPERA specifies three options for recovery audit services—recovery audits can be performed (1) within the agency itself, (2) by other U.S. departments and agencies, or (3) by a private sector entity. A-123 added a fourth option: by nonfederal entities that expend federal awards.[21] IPERA allows agencies flexibility in the type of contract they use to procure recovery audit services, including contingency contracts, in which private sector contractors receive a percentage of overpayments that the agency is able to collect as payment for their services.[22] However, certain types of payments recovered—amounts recovered due to interim improper payments made under ongoing contracts, recoveries from nondiscretionary appropriations, amounts recovered from unexpired appropriations, amongst others—cannot be used to pay contingency fee contracts. In these cases, agencies must establish alternative payment arrangements, such as through appropriations, to pay contractors.

A specific set of requirements and prohibitions governs the use of contracted payment recapture auditing firms. Contractors are required to provide semi-annual reports to the contracting agency on conditions giving rise to improper payments and recommendations for mitigation of these conditions; notify the agency of identified overpayments, regardless of whether they occurred at the contracting agency or another agency beyond the scope of the contract; and report credible evidence of fraud to the agency and its Office of Inspector General. In addition, contractors must familiarize themselves with agencies' policies and procedures and protect the confidentiality of sensitive financial information that could identify an individual. Payment recapture audit contractors are not prohibited from visiting the property of a payment recapture audit subject, though they cannot compel the production of records or information from the agency's contractors, nor can they act as agents for the federal government in the recovery of funds. Actual collection activities are carried out by federal agencies or nonfederal entities expending federal awards; a payment recapture audit contractor may only perform the collection activity if it is permitted by statute.

A-123 elaborates on IPERA's delineation of the disposition of amounts from nonexpired and expired discretionary funds. Overpayments recaptured from nonexpired discretionary funds, appropriated after the enactment of IPERA, must be returned to the appropriation from which they were made and not used for any other purpose. Overpayments from mandatory fund accounts, trust fund accounts, or special fund accounts must revert back to those accounts, as well. The distribution of any expired, recaptured discretionary collected amounts is at the discretion of agency heads, though amounts allocated to (1) the financial management improvement program, (2) the appropriation or fund from which the overpayment was made, or (3) inspector general activities are subject to maximum limits under IPERA. Within these constraints, agency heads may determine the actual percentages after reimbursing expenses for administering payment recapture audit programs and paying contractors for payment recapture audit services.

IPERA subjects agencies to two reporting requirements. First, it requires agencies to report annually on their payment recapture audit programs in their Performance and Accountability Reports (PARs) or Agency Financial Reports (AFRs). OMB's guidance on information to be included in these reports is consistent with IPERA, though it adds some additional requirements:[23]

- Provision of the total amount of payments subject to review, the actual amount of payments reviewed, the amounts identified for recapture, and the amounts actually recaptured in the current year; these amounts should be separated by those attributable to internal agency activities versus payment recapture audit contractors.
- Description and justification of the classes of payments excluded from payment recapture audit review by the agency.

Second, agencies using federal employees or external contractors must complete an additional annual report for OMB, Congress, and their inspectors general, containing recommendations from payment recapture auditors on mitigation of conditions that promote overpayments and corrective actions taken by the agency in response to these recommendations. It is due by November 1 each year and should describe recommendations and actions taken by the agency during the previous fiscal year.

## ANALYSIS

Agencies have had 10 years to implement improper payment legislation, beginning with the enactment of IPIA in 2002, which established the core requirements of improper payments reduction. IPERA, while enacted more recently, reinforced IPIA's core requirements and expanded agencies' responsibilities to prevent and recover improper payments. Therefore, it is possible to evaluate agency efforts in reducing payment error rates over several years, and to make an initial assessment of recovery audit programs.

**Table 1. Government-Wide Improper Payment Amounts and Rates (FY2004–FY2012) ($ amounts in billions)**

| | Improper Payment Amount ($) | Improper Payment Rate (%) |
|---|---|---|
| FY2004 | 45 | 4.35 |
| FY2005 | 38 | 3.14 |
| FY2006 | 41 | 2.91 |
| FY2007 | 42 | 2.81 |
| FY2008 | 73 | 3.95 |
| FY2009 | 105 | 5.42 |
| FY2010 | 121 | 5.29 |
| FY2011 | 115 | 4.69 |
| FY2012 | 108 | 4.35 |

Source: Improper payment amounts for FY2004-FY2012 in this table were constructed from the Office of Federal Financial Management's improper payments dataset. Amounts are approximate due to rounding.

## Improper Payments

The government's improper payment rate of 4.4% in FY2004—the first year of reporting required by IPIA—appears static when compared to the same rate for FY2012. Over time, though, the rate has declined to a low of 2.81% in FY2007 and reached a high of 5.42% in FY2009, as shown in **Table 1**.[24] As a consequence, agencies continue to make tens of billions of dollars a year in improper payments. Since the IPIA reporting requirements took effect, agencies have made over half a trillion dollars ($688 billion) in improper payments. In FY2012 alone the government made $108 billion in improper payments.[25]

The inability of the government to reduce its overall improper payment rate is partly due to agencies' failure to reduce substantially the error rates for risk-susceptible federal programs with multi-billion dollar annual outlays. In some cases, error rates for those programs have actually increased over time. Moreover, the full extent of the improper payment problem is not known because agencies have yet to develop improper payment rates for some programs, including programs which OMB estimates may have annual improper payments of at least $750 million annually.[26]

Agencies did not have improper payment estimates in place for all of their risk-susceptible programs and activities for the first year of IPIA reporting,

FY2004. Since then, agencies have expanded the number of programs reported each year as they develop valid improper payment estimates for them. During this same time, the annual dollar amount of improper payments reported has more than doubled, rising from $45 billion in FY2004 to $108 billion in FY2012.[27]

While the inclusion of additional programs accounts for much of the growth in improper payments reported since FY2004,[28] there are a number of multi-billion dollar programs which have seen little or no improvement in their improper payment rates, and in some cases the error rates for these programs have actually increased over time. The improper payment rate for the Medicare Fee-for-Service program, for example, increased from 5.2% in FY2005 to 8.5% in FY2012, and the amount of improper payments made under the program has more than doubled in that same period of time, increasing from $12 billion to approximately $30 billion.[29] Similarly, the improper payment rate for the Unemployment Insurance (UI) program increased from 10% in FY2005 to 11% in FY2012, and the amount of improper payments under UI increased from $3 billion to $10 billion.[30] Error rates—and improper payment amounts—have also increased over time for the Supplemental Security Income (SSI) program and Medicare Advantage (Part C).[31] While OMB has argued that administrative problems, such as the lack of required documentation, are the root causes of most improper payments,[32] this does not explain why a program's improper payment error rate would increase over time—particularly when agencies were to begin addressing these weaknesses 10 years ago with the enactment of IPIA.

### *Incomplete Scope*

The full scope of improper payments has not been determined because agencies have not yet developed estimates for all of their risk-susceptible programs or are re-calculating their initial estimates. Among these programs are several that have multi-billion dollar outlays and may have annual improper payment amounts in the hundreds of millions to billions of dollars. The Department of Health and Human Services (HHS), for example, is re-estimating its error rate for the Children's Health Insurance Program (CHIP). In FY2008, HHS initially reported an error rate of 14.7% for CHIP and outlays of $5.7 billion, resulting in $834 million in improper payments.[33] Similarly, the Federal Communications Commission (FCC) is re-estimating the improper payment rate for the High-Cost Program component of the Universal Service Fund (USF). The initial improper payment rate for the High-Cost Program, published for FY2007 expenditures, was 16.5%, and total outlays exceeded

$3.7 billion, resulting in $620 million in improper payments that year.[34] One of the largest risk-susceptible programs that lacks a valid improper payment error rate is the Earned Income Tax Credit (EITC), which is administered by the Department of the Treasury. The initial improper payment rate for the EITC, published for FY2004 expenditures, was 24.5%, with total outlays $39.4 billion, resulting in $9.7 billion in improper payments.[35] OMB estimates that the FY2011 improper payment rate for the EITC was between 21% and 26%, with a "rough" estimate of improper payments in excess of $15 billion.[36] Until these and all other risk-susceptible programs have valid improper payment rates, the extent of the problem will remain unknown.

### *Ineffective Internal Controls*

According to GAO, many agencies have not yet established internal controls that are effective enough to significantly reduce the risk of improper payments.[37] As noted, OMB has reported that the three most common causes of improper payments are administrative in nature, specifically due to agencies failing to (1) verify that recipient-reported information is accurate, such as whether a recipient is working; (2) ensure that requests for payments are for valid purposes, such as whether a claim for a particular medical service is necessary given the recipient's medical condition; and (3) have the required documentation for each recipient, such as a completed application for benefits.

To address these deficiencies, GAO has recommended that agencies to consider implementing a range of preventive controls, including technological tools.[38] Among these tools, GAO recommended that agencies share data to validate recipient eligibility from a variety of sources. HHS, for example, shares information from its New Hires database with the Department of Labor to confirm the employment status of an individual claiming benefits from the Unemployment Insurance program.[39] GAO also recommended that agencies utilize predictive analytic technologies, which identify unusual patterns or abnormalities in service utilization or billing that may indicate fraudulent activity.[40] Predictive analytic technology, for example, is currently employed by HHS to screen all claims under the Medicare Fee-for-Service program prior to payment. GAO is evaluating the effectiveness of the technology in preventing payments for fraudulent claims.[41]

GAO also recommended that agencies provide more extensive training tailored for the various parties involved in the lifecycle of a payment: agency staff, beneficiaries, and service providers (when applicable).[42] The training for agency staff, for example, might emphasize methods for detecting improper payments, while training for beneficiaries and service providers might focus on program requirements.

In addition, GAO reiterated the need for agency managers to ensure that audit findings are resolved in a timely manner.[43] Managers have three important responsibilities in this regard, according to GAO. First, they must promptly review any audit findings that show deficiencies in agency internal controls; second, they must determine the proper steps needed to resolve these deficiencies; and third, they must complete those steps within an established, expeditious time frame.[44]

## Recovery Audits

One argument advanced by the proponents of IPERA was that it would increase the recovery of overpayments.[45] OMB issued government-wide guidance on the implementation of IPERA in April 2011. However, only about seven months of IPERA's payment recapture audit provisions were in effect by the time agencies reported on improper payments in their FY2011 Agency Financial Reports (AFRs).[46] That said, IPERA may have had a positive impact on efforts to recoup overpayments. According to the Treasury Department, agencies recaptured more than $1.2 billion in improper payments to contractors and vendors in FY2011,[47] which is nearly double the $688 million recaptured in FY2010.[48]

A recent GAO report noted that some agencies have indicated that statutory or regulatory barriers have interfered with their ability to perform recovery audits.[49] GAO identified the Office of Personnel Management (OPM) and the Department of Agriculture (USDA) as specific cases in point. In its FY2011 AFR, OPM stated that current law and Treasury Department regulations prohibit financial institutions from providing the requisite information to recover overpayments for its Retirement Program.[50] The USDA cited Section 281[51] of the Agriculture Reorganization Act of 1994[52] as the chief impediment to conducting recovery audits for the Farm Service Agency (FSA) and Commodity Credit Corporation (CCC). Section 281 prohibits the recovery of incorrect payments after 90 days unless the participant believes the decision to be erroneous.[53]

Other agencies not cited in the GAO report have encountered problems, as well. The Department of Housing and Urban Development (HUD) explained that certain programs lack "the means to capture and report the amounts of improper payments identified and recovered."[54] The Department of Education (ED) cited the high burden of proof required to recover funds under the General Education Provisions Act (GEPA) as a barrier to recovery auditing.[55]

IPERA's cost-effectiveness requirement may limit the funds recovered through recovery audits. Under the law, agencies are required to conduct recovery audits only if so doing is cost-effective. If an agency determines that a recovery audit would not be cost-effective, it must notify the Office of Management and Budget (OMB) and its inspector general with the analysis it performed to reach this decision.

For FY2011, several agencies determined that recovery audits would not be cost-effective; two selected examples include the Treasury Department and the Small Business Administration (SBA). According to the Department of the Treasury's Office of Inspector General (OIG), neither the Treasury Executive Office for Asset Forfeiture (TEOAF) nor the Bureau of the Public Debt's Office of Public Debt Accounting (OPDA) performed recovery audits. The Treasury Department considered them low risk and immaterial and so deemed that recovery audits would not be cost- effective.[56] SBA cited low error rates and program complexity as reasons that payment audits would not be cost-effective. With regard to contracting specifically, for example, SBA stated that contracting's limited amount of outlays—$133.4 million over the improper payment period— meant that recovery audits would not be cost-effective.[57] Given that $133.4 million exceeded the $1 million threshold for conducting recovery audits under IPERA, SBA was required to provide a justification for this decision, but it did not.[58]

While OMB Circular A-123, Appendix C, instructs agencies on considerations they should take into account when evaluating whether a recovery audit would be cost-effective, there are no clear- cut criteria that would achieve a uniform response across agencies. Agency "opt-out" in the absence of definitive standards of cost-effectiveness could result in missed opportunities to recoup overpayments. In addition, understating amounts potentially available for recovery could limit congressional oversight, as incomplete and incorrect information might impede effective program monitoring and review.

# IMPROPER PAYMENTS ELIMINATION AND RECOVERY AUDIT IMPROVEMENT ACT OF 2012

In an attempt to expand the scope of data used to verify that payments are being made to eligible recipients and for the correct amount, Congress passed the Improper Payments Elimination and Recovery Audit Improvement Act of 2012 (IPERIA; P.L. 112-248). IPERIA is in the early stages of implementation—President Obama signed it into law on January 10, 2013—so there is no evidence yet as to the law's effectiveness in reducing improper payments and increasing the amounts recovered. The following section describes key provisions and provides a brief analysis of the potential benefits of the law.

## Improper Payments

IPERIA requires OMB to identify a list of "high-priority" federal programs for greater levels of oversight. These programs must be chosen on the basis of the relatively high dollar value or error rate of improper payments, or because they are deemed more susceptible to improper payments when compared to other high-risk programs, regardless of size. OMB is also required to establish annual targets, as well as quarterly and semi-annual actions for reducing improper payments for the high-priority programs. In addition, each agency with a high-priority program is required to submit an annual report on the steps agencies have taken, and plan to take, to prevent and recover future improper payments. The report will be submitted to the inspector general of the agency and posted on a website accessible to the public. The inspector general, in turn, must submit a report to Congress that assesses the quality of the improper payment estimates for each high-priority program, determines whether proper controls are in place to identify and prevent future improper payments, and makes recommendations to Congress on how agency plans might be modified to improve their improper payment estimates and internal controls.

IPERIA also requires OMB to issue new guidance intended to increase the accuracy of agency improper payment estimates. The bill

- establishes new standards for sampling payments;
- bars agencies from relying on self-reporting by recipients for estimates;
- requires agencies to include all improper payments in their estimates, including those payments recovered or in the process of being recovered; and
- includes payments to employees in their estimates.

In addition, IPERIA requires a "Do Not Pay Initiative" similar to the "Do Not Pay List" established by President Barack Obama.[59] Under IPERIA, agencies are required to verify recipient eligibility by reviewing available databases prior to issuing a payment or award. At a minimum, agencies must verify eligibility by reviewing data in the

- Death Master File, maintained by the Social Security Administration;
- Excluded Parties List System, maintained by the General Services Administration;
- Debt Check Database, maintained by the Department of the Treasury;
- Credit Alert System, maintained by the Department of Housing and Urban Development; and
- List of Excluded Parties and Entities, maintained by the inspector general of the Department of Health and Human Services.

IPERIA gives OMB the authority to include additional databases as part of the "Do Not Pay Initiative," as long as the public is provided notice and opportunity to comment before the database is included. OMB must issue a report to Congress each year that evaluates agency efforts to implement the "Do Not Pay Initiative," including whether the initiative has led to reduced improper payments and the identification of incorrect data.

To facilitate data integration across agencies, IPERIA requires OMB to submit a plan by March 11, 2013, for (1) including other databases in the "Do Not Pay Initiative"; (2) maximizing agency access to the databases; and (3) developing agreements between agency inspectors general that would permit data sharing. OMB is required to issue guidance on the IG agreements, including standards for reimbursement of costs associated with implementation, retention and destruction of records, and privacy protections. Thirty days after OMB submits its plan, it is required to ensure that a working data-sharing system is in place, although it only needs to include three agencies by that deadline. By June 1, 2013, all agencies must review all their payments for all programs through the initiative.

In addition to drawing on data from existing sources, IPERIA requires the Attorney General to submit a report to Congress within a year of enactment that would assess the ability of using state, local, and federal incarceration status as a method for identifying and preventing improper payments. IPERIA also requires the Social Security Administration (SSA) to take steps to improve the accuracy and timeliness of death data maintained by SSA.

## Recovery Audits

Under IPERA, agencies must establish annual payment recapture targets for their programs. By FY2013, the proportion of recovered amounts to amounts identified for recovery must be at least 0.85 (that is, a recovery rate of at least 85%). IPERIA expands upon these provisions by requiring the Director of OMB to set recovery targets for improper payments, with specific amounts identified for recovery audit contractors. In addition, the legislation requires the Director of OMB to determine both current and historical improper payments recovery amounts and rates, including those recaptured by recovery audit contractors, and provide a list of agency recovery audit contract programs.[60]

## Initial Analysis

IPERIA's provisions target areas for improvement that are known to be weak, particularly with regard to developing more accurate improper payment estimates.[61] In addition, the explicit requirement to include payments to federal employees when estimating improper payments may yield new areas for savings, as OMB has reported that federal benefit programs may be susceptible to high rates of improper payments—perhaps over $1 billion a year. In FY2008, for example, the Office of Personnel Management reported more than $330 million in improper payments for federal health, life, and retirement programs,[62] and the Department of Defense reported more than $730 million in improper payments for military and civilian pay, health, and retirement programs.[63] Finally, the ability of agencies to access data from a range of sources across the government may prove to be a valuable tool for preventing payments to ineligible recipients. It may be useful, however, to compare the cost of integrating and improving existing data sources, as IPERIA requires, to the potential savings generated by doing so.

## S. 1360: IMPROPER PAYMENTS AGENCY COOPERATION ENHANCEMENT ACT OF 2013

On May 8, 2013, the Senate Committee on Homeland Security and Governmental Affairs held a hearing on eliminating improper payments to people who have already died.[64] IPERIA included provisions that were intended to address this problem—the law requires agencies to check SSA's Death Master File (DMF) to ensure intended recipients are still alive before issuing payments.[65] A report by the Government Accountability Office (GAO), however, determined that DMF data were flawed and that many improper payments to decedents were going undetected.[66] Senator Carper, committee chairman, called the problem "frustrating but solvable" and stated that he wanted the hearing to result in steps that the government could take to ensure agencies receive the most accurate information from the DMF.[67]

According to Daniel Bertoni, GAO director of Education, Workforce, and Income Security Issues, who testified at the hearing, the accuracy of the DMF is uncertain because SSA does not verify all of the death reports it receives.[68] Multiple sources report deaths to SSA, some of which SSA considers "highly accurate" and others that SSA considers "less accurate." SSA reviews each file submitted from a "less accurate" source before recording an individual as deceased in the DMF. The "less accurate" sources include post offices, financial institutions, the Department of Veterans Affairs, and the Centers for Medicare and Medicaid Services. SSA does not verify death reports from "highly accurate" sources before recording an individual as deceased in the DMF. The "highly accurate" sources include data from states reported through the Electronic Death Registration System (EDRS), family members, and funeral directors. Regardless of the source, SSA does not verify deaths reported for non-beneficiaries. If a post office submitted a death report to SSA, for example, the death would be recorded in the DMF without verification if the decedent was not receiving SSA benefits. Bertoni did not provide an estimate of how many DMF files are inaccurate.

Bertoni also discussed the degree to which agencies utilize the DMF. As noted, SSA receives death data from state governments. The Social Security Act, however, prohibits SSA from sharing state data with federal agencies that do not pay benefits. SSA, therefore, must determine whether an agency is eligible for access to the full DMF on a case-by-case basis. As of May 8, 2013, SSA had granted full access to only six federal agencies, all of which make benefit payments:

- Centers for Medicare and Medicaid Services (CMS)
- Department of Defense (DOD)
- Department of Veterans Affairs (VA)
- Internal Revenue Service (IRS)
- Office of Personnel Management (OPM)
- Railroad Retirement Board (RRB)

Agencies are generally required to reimburse SSA for the "reasonable cost of sharing the [DMF] data." Despite this, Bertoni noted that SSA is not reimbursed by all agencies for access to the full DMF. The VA is statutorily exempt from paying SSA, so it does not reimburse SSA at all. Neither does OPM, which has an arrangement with SSA under which the agencies exchange information at no cost to either party. CMS and DOD do reimburse SSA, but at different amounts.

Other federal agencies—including some that pay benefits—purchase only the partial DMF. These agencies include the Departments of Labor, Agriculture, and Justice. The partial DMF excludes data provided by states—estimated at about 11 million death reports. The agencies that pay benefits may be eligible for access to the full DMF, but they have not requested access. Bertoni did not explain why some benefit-paying agencies had not requested access to the full DMF.

## S. 1360

In response to issues raised at the May 8, 2013, hearing, Chairman Carper introduced S. 1360, the Improper Payments Agency Cooperation Enhancement Act of 2013. The bill's provisions, discussed below, are directed at improving the accuracy of, and increasing access to, DMF data.

### *Registry Access and Data Quality*

S. 1360 would require the SSA Commissioner (Commissioner) to establish a National Deaths Registry (Registry) that must include information agencies need to fully implement IPERIA. The Commissioner would also be required to enter into agreements with federal agencies that would enable them to have full access to all of the death data in the Registry. Agencies would be required to reimburse the Commissioner for the reasonable cost of carrying out the agreement. The Commissioner would also be required to enter into similar agreements with state, local, and tribal governments, "to the extent feasible." The agreements would help them prevent, identify, and recover improper payments made under federally funded programs. These agreements, like those made with federal agencies, would require state, local, or tribal governments to reimburse the Commissioner for access to the Registry.

The bill would also require the Commissioner to implement procedures for

- identifying and correcting errors, including those identified by members of the public;
- determining the accuracy of death records in the Registry;
- ensuring that the Registry is operated and maintained according to best practices for privacy, security, and disclosure; and
- providing data to contractors that have been certified by a federal agency, or state, local, or tribal government, as being compliant with applicable privacy and security protocols.

The Commissioner would be given the specific authority to share all of the information in the Registry with any federal agency, including data received from states. This provision would supersede the language in the Social Security Act that prohibits the Commissioner from sharing state data with federal agencies that do not provide benefits.

***Reporting Data to the Registry***

S. 1360 would require the Director of the Office of Management and Budget (Director) to identify agencies that have data which might be used for matching data in the Registry. If an agency has data on annuity recipients, for example, the Director must establish a method for comparing the data the agency has with the data in the Registry. The Commissioner would then use the comparison to confirm the accuracy and completeness of the Registry data, and to identify conflicting data that needs to be further researched. Each agency identified by the Director would be required to submit to the Commissioner, on a regular basis, data relating to the death of a federal beneficiary, federal annuitant recipient, or other individual that might be in the

Registry. The Director would be required to submit a plan to Congress that explains how state, local, and tribal governments will use data matching to improve the accuracy of data in the Registry and in their own databases.

***Sharing Data***

S. 1360 would require the U.S. Postal Service to provide agencies access to delivery addresses, including a list of known locations of commercial mailboxes. The Postal Service has the authority to request reimbursement from agencies that use this data. In addition, federal agencies with data that pertain to federal beneficiaries or annuitants must share that data with other agencies.

***Data Analytics***

S. 1360 would require the Secretary of the Treasury, within 180 days of enactment, to submit a report to Congress which includes a description of any analysis or investigation of data used to implement the "Do Not Pay Initiative." Examples include matching data in the Registry to state beneficiary enrollment lists, and comparing program data from multiple agencies to identify payment duplication. The Secretary of the Treasury would also be required to describe the metrics used to determine whether data analytics reduced improper payments.

***Task Force on Federal Annuitants***

S. 1360 would require the OMB Director to assemble a task force of agencies to reduce payments to deceased federal annuitants. To that end, the task force would be a forum to share best practices for identifying deceased annuitants and to improve data-sharing among agencies. The task force must include representatives from four agencies: DOD, SSA, VA, and OPM. In addition, the task force must include any other agency that provides or conducts oversight of annuities.

***Analysis of S. 1360***

S. 1360 includes provisions that, if fully implemented, may improve the accuracy of death data, which in turn may reduce improper payments to deceased individuals. Expanding data matching with state, local, and tribal governments, for example, would provide new sources of information against which the data in the Registry could be compared. Participation in data sharing, however, comes with a cost. The Department of Defense, for example, pays $40,000 a year for access to the Registry.[69] It is not known how many state, local, and tribal governments would be able to obtain the funds needed to reimburse SSA for access to the Registry.

As noted, the Electronic Death Registration System (EDRS) is considered a "highly accurate" source of data for the Registry. As of March 2013, however, only 35 states submitted their death reports using EDRS.[70] SSA estimates that with the necessary funding, EDRS could be implemented in the remaining states within four years.[71] One option for improving the quality and quantity of death data in the Registry would be to consider funding the implementation of EDRS nation-wide. Among the questions that might be asked to assist Congress in this decision are

- Do the states without EDRS have the capacity to implement it without a major technology upgrade?
- Would states contribute to the cost of implementing EDRS?
- How long would it take for the government to recover its investment in EDRS expansion through the prevention and recovery of improper payments?

S. 1360 includes language that would permit SSA to share state death data with federal agencies that do not issue benefit payments—agencies that are currently prohibited from accessing state death data by the Social Security Act. Agencies may discover similar statutory obstacles as they try to formalize data sharing agreements, as required by S. 1360. One option for identifying these statutory obstacles and making them known to Congress would be to require the Secretary of the Treasury to include them in its report on data analytics. S. 1360 requires the Secretary to submit a report within 180 days of enactment that includes a description of "multiple agencies and programs for which comparison of data could show payment duplication." As part of that review, the Secretary could be required to work with agencies to determine whether any statutory barriers to sharing that data exist. Another option would be to require the OMB Director to include statutory barriers in its annual report on the implementation of S. 1360. The first such annual report would be required not more than one year after the enactment of S. 1360.

## End Notes

[1] P.L. 107-107 is the National Defense Authorization Act of FY2002. Section 831 of P.L. 107-107 is commonly referred to as the Recovery Audit Act of 2002.

[2] Government Accountability Office, *Status of Agencies' Efforts to Address Improper Payment and Recovery Auditing Requirements*, GAO-08-438T, January 31, 2008.

[3] 31 U.S.C. §1532.

[4] IPERA does not define the term "recovery audit."

[5] Office of Management and Budget, *OMB Circular A-123, Appendix C (Revised)*, April 14, 2011, at http://www.whitehouse.gov/sites/default/files/omb/memoranda/2011/m11-16.pdf.

[6] In the 112th Congress, Senator Tom Carper is the chairman of the Senate Subcommittee on Federal Financial Management, Government Information, Federal Services, and International Security, which held this hearing.

[7] U.S. Congress, Senate Committee on Homeland Security and Governmental Affairs, Subcommittee on Federal Financial Management, Government Information, Federal Services, and International Security, *Eliminating Agency Payment Errors*, 110th Cong., 2nd sess., January 31, 2008, S. Hrg. 110-501 (Washington: GPO, 2008), p. 4.

[8] IPERA does not provide a definition for "program" or "activity." OMB guidance on the implementation of IPERA states that "program and activity" is referred to as "program," and programs include grants, benefits, loans, and contract programs. See Office of Management and Budget, *OMB Circular A-123, Appendix C (Revised)*, April 14, 2011, at http://www.whitehouse.gov/sites/default/files/omb/memoranda/2011/m11-16.pdf.

[9] This law repealed that which established initial recovery audit requirements (P.L. 107-107).

[10] Entities may include persons (IPERA at 124 Stat. 2229).

[11] The aging schedule of outstanding amounts shows the amount of overpayments that have been identified through a payment recapture audit program but not yet recovered. Aging typically begins at the time when an overpayment has been detected. For a table template, see Table 4 in Office of Management and Budget, *Financial Reporting Requirements*, August 3, 2012, p. 157, at http://www.whitehouse.gov/sites/default/files/omb/assets/omb/circulars/a136/a136_revised_2012.pdf

[12] The legislation does not indicate where the report was to be submitted. In the section on reporting the statistically valid estimates, it states that these estimates should be included in the materials accompanying the annual financial statement of the agency. OMB guidance on the implementation of IPERA states that agencies must report annually on their payment recapture program in their Performance and Accountability Reports (PARs) and Agency Financial Reports (AFRs). See Office of Management and Budget, *OMB Circular A-123, Appendix C (Revised)*, April 14, 2011, at http://www.whitehouse.gov/sites/default/files/omb/memoranda/2011/m11-16.pdf.

[13] As of December 15, 2012, CRS could not locate this report.

[14] Office of Management and Budget, *Circular A-123, Management's Responsibility for Internal Control*, December 21, 2004, at http://www.whitehouse.gov/omb/circulars_a123_rev.

[15] OMB uses the term "program" to refer to both programs and activities in Appendix C of A-123.

[16] Recapture activities are designed to identify and recover overpayments identified by a payment recapture audit or post-award audit. A post-award audit is defined in the guidance as a "post-award examination of the accounting and financial records of a payment recipient that is performed by an agency official, or an authorized representative of the agency official." A post-award audit differs from a payment recapture audit in that a post-award audit is conducted to assess compliance with the terms of an award or contract, whereas a recovery audit is intended to identify overpayments.

[17] IPERA's recovery audit provisions are limited to overpayments.

[18] Agencies may also consider the likelihood that expected recoveries will exceed the costs associated with identifying overpayments. This hinges on the availability of tools that can efficiently perform the recovery audits and whether such tools can be employed to identify significant overpayments in lieu of labor-intensive techniques.

[19] The first reporting year is FY2011, the second is FY2012, and the third is FY2013.

[20] Under IPERA, up to 25% of funds recovered through a payment recapture audit program may be dedicated to financial management improvement programs, a portion of which may be distributed to state and local governments for these purposes.

[21] A nonfederal entity is a state, local government, or non-profit organization. Defined in Office of Management and Budget, *OMB Circular A-133: Audits of States, Local Governments, and Non-Profit Organizations*, June 30, 1997, at http://www.whitehouse.gov/sites/default/files/omb/assets/a133/a133_revised_2007.pdf.

[22] Under these contracts, recoveries must be collected by the agency before payments to contractors are rendered.

[23] This accompanies the requirement discussed previously in which the agency must advise OMB and the agency's Inspector General of the decision not to conduct a payment recapture audit if it would not be cost-effective. The PAR or AFR should contain a list of programs and activities for which a payment recapture audit was determined not to be cost-effective, and a description of the justifications and analysis used in making that determination.

[24] Office of Management and Budget, *Improper Payment Rates Across the Federal Government (FYs 2004-2012),* PaymentAccuracy.gov, at http://paymentaccuracy.gov/tabular-data/govt-wide-improper-rates.

[25] Office of Management and Budget, *About Improper Payments*, PaymentAccuracy.gov, at http://www.paymentaccuracy.gov/about-improper-payments.

[26] Office of Management and Budget, *Programs Not Reported,* PaymentAccuracy.gov, at http://paymentaccuracy.gov/ content/programs-not-reported.

[27] FY2004 improper payment amount: Office of Federal Financial Management, Office of Management and Budget. *Improper Payments Dataset*, at http://www.whitehouse.gov/omb/financial/improper_payment_dataset. FY2012 improper payment amount: Office of Management and Budget, *About Improper Payments*, PaymentAccuracy.gov, at http://www.paymentaccuracy.gov/about-improper-payments.

[28] GAO has attributed increases in aggregate improper payment amounts over time to newly reported programs or increases in improper payments in specific programs. On newly reported programs, see Government Accountability Office, *Improper Payments: Agencies' Efforts to Address Improper Payment and Recovery Auditing Requirements Continue*, GAO- GAO-07-635T, March 2007, p. 8, at http://www.gao.gov/assets/120/116089.pdf. On increases in specific programs, see Government Accountability Office, *Improper Payments: Recent Efforts to Address Improper Payments and Remaining Challenges*, GAO-11-575, April 2011, p. 5, at http://www.gao.gov/new.items/d11575t.pdf.

[29] Office of Management and Budget, *Historical Improper Payment Rates for Medicare Fee-for-Service*, PaymentAccuracy.gov, at http://www.paymentaccuracy.gov/tabular-data/historical-by-program/186.

[30] In FY2010, UI reported an improper payment amount of nearly $18 billion. Office of Management and Budget, *Historical Improper Payment Rates for Unemployment Insurance (UI)*, PaymentAccuracy.gov, at http://www.paymentaccuracy.gov/tabular-data/historical-by-program/358.

[31] Office of Management and Budget, *Supplemental Security Income (SSI)*, PaymentAccuracy.gov, at http://www.paymentaccuracy.gov/programs/supplemental-security-income; and Office of Management and Budget, *Medicare Advantage (Part C)*, PaymentAccuracy.gov, at http://www.paymentaccuracy.gov/programs/medicare-advantage-part-c.

[32] Office of Management and Budget, *About Improper Payments*, PaymentAccuracy.gov, at http://paymentaccuracy.gov/about-improper-payments.

[33] Office of Management and Budget, *Improving the Accuracy and Integrity of Federal Payments*, January 8, 2009, p. 21, at http://www.whitehouse.gov/sites/default/files/omb/assets/about_omb/2008_ipia_final.pdf.

[34] Ibid., p. 23.

[35] Ibid., p. 24.

[36] Office of Management and Budget, *Earned Income Tax Credit (EITC)*, PaymentAccuracy.gov, at http://www.paymentaccuracy.gov/tracked/earned-income-tax-credit-eitc-2012.

[37] Government Accountability Office, *Improper Payments: Remaining Challenges and Strategies for Governmentwide Reduction Efforts*, GAO-12-573T, March 2012, p. 11, at http://www.gao.gov/assets/590/589681.pdf.

[38] Ibid., p. 22.

[39] Ibid., p. 23.

[40] Ibid., p. 23.

[41] Ibid., p. 23.

[42] Ibid., p. 24.

[43] Ibid., p. 24.

[44] Ibid., p. 24.

[45] For example, see Sen. Thomas Carper, remarks in the Senate, *Congressional Record*, vol. 156, part 104 (July 14, 2010), p. S5809.

[46] For example, the Department of the Treasury's FY2011 AFR noted, "Due to the delayed release of IPERA implementation guidance, Treasury's bureaus were not able to fully implement or develop the mechanisms to acquire the additional information specified in the amended Payment Recapture Audit guidance." Department of the Treasury, *Agency Financial Report, Fiscal Year 2011*, November 15, 2011, p. 161, http://www.treasury.gov/about/budget-performance/annual-performance-plan/Documents/FY 2011 AFR-Final Version.pdf. OMB provided interim guidance on November 16, 2010. See OMB, "Increasing Efforts to Recapture Improper Payments by Intensifying and Expanding Payment Recapture Audits," Memorandum for Heads of Executive Departments and Agencies from Danny Werfel and Daniel I. Gordon, November 16, 2010, M-11-04.

[47] Department of the Treasury, *2011 Financial Report of the United States Government*, December 2011, at http://www.fms.treas.gov/fr/11frusg/11frusg.pdf.

[48] Office of Management and Budget, *Government-wide Improper Payments Recaptured (Billions)*, Performance.gov, at http://finance.performance.gov/content/initiative-recapture-improper-payments-508. According to PaymentAccuracy.gov, the increase from FY2010 to FY2011 is over 80%. See Office of Management and Budget, *About Improper Payments*, PaymentAccuracy.gov, at http://www.paymentaccuracy.gov.

[49] Government Accountability Office, *Improper Payments: Remaining Challenges and Strategies for Governmentwide Reduction Efforts*, GAO-12-573T, March 28, 2012, at http://www.gao.gov/assets/590/589681.pdf.

[50] The Social Security Administration (SSA), the Railroad Retirement Board (RRB), and the Department of Veterans Affairs (VA) are exempted from these restrictions, as specified in law. Office of Personnel Management, *Agency Financial Report, Fiscal Year 2011*, November 2011, at http://www.opm.gov/gpra/opmgpra/2011_AFR.pdf.

[51] According to the Department of Agriculture, "[T]his statute is commonly referred to as the 'Finality Rule'." Department of Agriculture, *Department of Agriculture's Consolidated Financial Statements for Fiscal Years 2011 and 2010*, November 2011, p. 220, at http://www.usda.gov/oig/webdocs/50401-0001-11.pdf.

[52] P.L. 103-354; 108 Stat. 3209.

[53] Department of Agriculture, *Department of Agriculture's Consolidated Financial Statements for Fiscal Years 2011 and 2010*, November 2011, at http://www.usda.gov/oig/webdocs/50401-0001-11.pdf.

[54] Department of Housing and Urban Development, *Agency Financial Report, Fiscal Year 2011*, November 15, 2011, p. 182, at http://portal.hud.gov/huddoc/AFR2011.pdf.

[55] Department of Education, *FY 2011 Agency Financial Report*, November 15, 2011, at http://www2.ed.gov/about/ reports/annual/2011report/agency-financial-report.pdf.

[56] Nor did Treasury notify OMB or its OIG. The OIG report notes that the materiality threshold is not up to the agency and that notification is required for all programs with expenditures of at least $1 million regardless of the agency's opinion on materiality. Office of Inspector

General, Department of the Treasury, *Audit Report: Treasury Was Not in Compliance With IPERA for Fiscal Year 2011 (OIG-12-044)*, March 15, 2012, p. 6, at http://www.treasury.gov/about/organizational-structure/ig/Agency Documents/OIG12044 (web copy).pdf.

[57] Small Business Administration, *Agency Financial Report, Fiscal Year 2011*, November 15, 2011, at http://www.sba.gov/sites/default/files/Agency Financial Report FY 2011_0.pdf.

[58] Office of Inspector General, Small Business Administration, "Advisory Memorandum: The SBA's Improper Payment Review and Reporting for its Contracting Activities did not Comply with IPERA and IPIA Requirements During FY 2011 (Report No. 12-07)," March 8, 2012, at http://www.sba.gov/sites/default/files/Report 12-07 IPERA and IPIA review.pdf.

[59] The "Do Not Pay List" is a network of databases that contain information on a recipient's eligibility to receive federal benefits payments or federal awards, such as grants and contracts. Barack Obama, "Enhancing Payment Accuracy Through a 'Do Not Pay List'," 75 *Federal Register* 120, pp. 35953-35954, June 23, 2010, at http://www.gpo.gov/fdsys/pkg/FR-2010-06-23/pdf/2010-15412.pdf.

[60] Agencies report current-year information on recaptured amounts and rates, as well as cumulative recoveries, in their AFRs. OMB Circular A-123 requires agencies to separate reportable information resulting from internal recovery audits from that uncovered by recovery audit contractors.

[61] Government Accountability Office, *Improper Payments: Remaining Challenges and Strategies for Governmentwide Reduction Efforts*, GAO-12-573T, March 28, 2012, p. 10, at http://www.gao.gov/assets/590/589681.pdf.

[62] Office of Personnel Management, *Agency Financial Report, Fiscal Year 2008*, November 17, 2008, p. 134, at http://www.opm.gov/gpra/opmgpra/par2008/par2008.pdf.

[63] Department of Defense, *Fiscal Year 2008 Agency Financial Report*, November 17, 2008, p. 133, at http://comptroller.defense.gov/afr/fy2008/ Fiscal_Year_2008_Department_of_Defense_Agency_Wide_Financial_Statements_and_Notes.pdf.

[64] U.S. Congress, Senate Committee on Homeland Security and Governmental Affairs, *Curbing Federal Agency Waste and Fraud: New Steps to Strengthen the Integrity of Federal Payments*, hearing, 113th Cong., 1st sess., May 8, 2013, at http://www.hsgac.senate.gov/hearings/curbing-federal-agency-waste-and-fraud-new-steps-to-strengthen-the-integrity- of-federal-payments.

[65] 126 Stat. 2393.

[66] U.S. Government Accountability Office, *Social Security Administration: Preliminary Observations on the Death Master File*, GAO-13-574T, May 8, 2013, pp. 3-7.

[67] Testimony of U.S. Senator Tom Carper, in U.S. Congress, Chairman, Senate Committee on Homeland Security and Governmental Affairs, *Curbing Federal Agency Waste and Fraud: New Steps to Strengthen the Integrity of Federal Payments*, hearing, 113th Cong., 1st sess., May 8, 2013, at http://www.hsgac.senate.gov/hearings/curbing-federal- agency-waste-and-fraud-new-steps-to-strengthen-the-integrity-of-federal-payments.

[68] Testimony of GAO Director of Education, Workforce, and Income Security Issues, Daniel Bertoni, in U.S. Congress, Chairman, Senate Committee on Homeland Security and Governmental Affairs, *Curbing Federal Agency Waste and Fraud: New Steps to Strengthen the Integrity of Federal Payments*, hearing, 113th Cong., 1st sess., May 8, 2013, at http://www.hsgac.senate.gov/hearings/curbing-federal-agency-waste-and-fraud-new-steps-to-strengthen-the-integrity- of-federal-payments.

[69] U.S. Government Accountability Office, *Social Security Administration: Preliminary Observations on the Death Master File*, GAO-13-574T, May 8, 2013, p. 8.

[70] U.S. Government Accountability Office, *Social Security Administration: Preliminary Observations on the Death Master File*, GAO-13-574T, May 8, 2013, p. 4.

[71] Testimony of Social Security Administration Inspector General Patrick P. O'Carroll, Jr., in U.S. Congress, Senate Committee on Homeland Security and Governmental Affairs, *Curbing Federal Agency Waste and Fraud: New Steps to Strengthen the Integrity of Federal Payments*, hearing, 113th Cong., 1st sess., May 8, 2013, at http://www.hsgac.senate.

gov/hearings/curbing-federal-agency-waste-and-fraud-new-steps-to-strengthen-the-integrity- of-federal-payments.

In: Improper Payments ...
Editor: Jeffrey B. Powers

ISBN: 978-1-62948-844-8


*Chapter 2*

# IMPROPER PAYMENTS: REMAINING CHALLENGES AND STRATEGIES FOR GOVERNMENTWIDE REDUCTION EFFORTS. TESTIMONY OF BERYL H. DAVIS, DIRECTOR, FINANCIAL MANAGEMENT AND ASSURANCE, GOVERNMENT ACCOUNTABILITY OFFICE*

***United States Government Accountability Office***

## WHY GAO DID THIS STUDY

Over the past decade, GAO has issued numerous reports and testimonies highlighting improper payment issues across the federal government as well as at specific agencies. Fiscal year 2011 marked the eighth year of implementation of the Improper Payments Information Act of 2002 (IPIA), as

* This is an edited, reformatted and augmented version of a Highlights of GAO-12-573T, a testimony before the Subcommittee on Federal Financial Management, Government Information, Federal Services, and International Security, Committee on Homeland Security and Governmental Affairs, U.S. Senate, dated March 28, 2012.

well as the first year of implementation for the Improper Payments Elimination and Recovery Act of 2010 (IPERA). IPIA requires executive branch agencies to annually identify programs and activities susceptible to significant improper payments, estimate the amount of improper payments for such programs and activities, and report these estimates along with actions taken to reduce them. IPERA amended IPIA and expanded requirements for recovering overpayments across a broad range of federal programs.

This testimony addresses (1) federal agencies' reported progress in estimating and reducing improper payments; (2) challenges in meeting current requirements to estimate and evaluate improper payments, including the results of GAO's case study of the estimation methodology and corrective actions for the Foster Care program; and (3) possible strategies that can be taken to move forward in reducing improper payments. This testimony is primarily based on prior GAO reports, including the report released today on improper payment estimates in the Foster Care program. It also includes unaudited improper payment information recently presented in federal entities' fiscal year 2011 performance and accountability reports and agency financial reports.

## What GAO Found

Federal agencies reported an estimated $115.3 billion in improper payments in fiscal year 2011, a decrease of $5.3 billion from the prior year reported estimate of $120.6 billion. According to the Office of Management and Budget (OMB), the $115.3 billion estimate was attributable to 79 programs spread among 17 agencies. Ten programs accounted for about $107 billion or 93 percent of the total estimated improper payments agencies reported. The reported decrease in fiscal year 2011 was primarily related to 3 programs—decreases in program outlays for the Unemployment Insurance program, and decreases in reported error rates for the Earned Income Tax Credit program and the Medicare Advantage program. Further, OMB reported that agencies recaptured $1.25 billion in improper payments to contractors and vendors.

The federal government continues to face challenges in determining the full extent of improper payments. Some agencies have not reported estimates for all risk-susceptible programs, while other agencies' estimation methodologies were found to be not statistically valid. For example, GAO's recently completed study of Foster Care improper payments found that the Administration for Children and Families (ACF) had established a process to calculate a national improper payment estimate for the Foster Care program, which totaled about $73 million for fiscal year 2010, the year covered by GAO's review. However, the estimate was not based on a statistically valid methodology and consequently did not provide a reasonably accurate estimate of the extent of Foster Care improper payments. Further, GAO found that ACF could not reliably assess the extent to which corrective actions reduced Foster Care improper payments.

A number of strategies are under way across government to help advance improper payment reduction goals. For example,

- Additional information and analysis on the root causes of improper payment estimates will assist agencies in targeting effective corrective actions and implementing preventive measures. Although agencies were required to report the root causes of improper payments in three categories beginning in fiscal year 2011, of the 79 programs with improper payment estimates that year, 42 programs reported the root cause information using the required categories.
- Implementing strong preventive controls can help defend against improper payments, increasing public confidence and avoiding the difficult "pay and chase" aspects of recovering improper payments. Preventive controls involve activities such as up-front validation of eligibility using data sharing, predictive analytic technologies, and training programs. Further, addressing program design issues, such as complex eligibility requirements, may also warrant further consideration.
- Effective detection techniques to quickly identify and recover improper payments are also important to a successful reduction strategy. Detection activities include data mining and recovery auditing. Another area for further exploration is the broader use of incentives to encourage states in efforts to implement effective detective controls.

Continuing work to implement and enhance these strategies will be needed to effectively reduce federal government improper payments.

Chairman Carper, Ranking Member Brown, and Members of the Subcommittee:

Thank you for the opportunity to be here today to discuss the issue of improper payments in federal programs and activities, including efforts by federal agencies to identify and reduce improper payments.[1] As the steward of taxpayer dollars, the federal government is accountable for how its agencies and grantees spend hundreds of billions of taxpayer dollars annually, including safeguarding those expenditures against improper payments, and establishing mechanisms to recover any overpayments. It is important to note that not all of the reported improper payment estimates represent a loss to the government. For example, such estimates include payments where there is insufficient documentation or a lack of documentation. Over the past decade, we have issued numerous reports and testimonies highlighting improper payment issues across the federal government as well as at specific agencies.[2] As requested by the Subcommittee, we recently completed our study of the improper payment estimation methodology and related corrective actions for the Department of Health and Human Services' (HHS) Foster Care program administered by the Administration for Children and Families (ACF).[3]

Today, my testimony will focus on

- federal agencies' reported progress in estimating and reducing improper payments;
- challenges in meeting current requirements to estimate and evaluate improper payments, including those identified through our case study of the estimation methodology used by HHS's Foster Care program;[4] and
- possible improper payment reduction strategies.

In preparing this statement, we drew primarily upon previously issued work related to (1) our fiscal year 2011 audit of the *Financial Report of the United States Government*,[5] (2) our report released today on improper payment estimates at HHS's Foster Care program,6 and (3) our other previously issued products dealing with improper payments. Our previous products are listed at the end of this statement. That work was conducted in accordance with generally accepted government auditing standards. We are also including unaudited improper payment information that federal entities reported in their fiscal year 2011 performance and accountability reports (PAR), agency financial reports (AFR), or other annual reporting.

# BACKGROUND

## Improper Payments Information Act of 2002

Fiscal year 2011 marked the eighth year of implementation of the Improper Payments Information Act of 2002 (IPIA),[7] as well as the first year of implementation for the Improper Payments Elimination and Recovery Act of 2010 (IPERA).[8] IPIA requires executive branch agencies to annually review all programs and activities to identify those that are susceptible to significant improper payments, estimate the annual amount of improper payments for such programs and activities, and report these estimates along with actions taken to reduce improper payments for programs with estimates that exceed \$10 million. IPERA, enacted July 22, 2010, amended IPIA by expanding on the previous requirements for identifying, estimating, and reporting on programs and activities susceptible to significant improper payments and expanding requirements for recovering overpayments across a broad range of federal programs.[9] IPERA included a new, broader requirement for agencies to conduct recovery audits, where cost effective, for each program and activity with at least \$1 million in annual program outlays. This IPERA provision significantly lowers the threshold for required recovery audits from \$500 million[10] to \$1 million and expands the scope for recovery audits to all programs and activities. Another IPERA provision calls for federal agencies' inspectors general to annually determine whether their respective agencies are in compliance with key IPERA requirements and to report on their determinations. Under Office of Management and Budget (OMB) implementing guidance, federal agencies are required to complete these reports within 120 days of the publication of their annual PARs or AFRs, with the fiscal year 2011 reports for most agencies due on March 15, 2012.

OMB continues to play a key role in the oversight of the governmentwide improper payments issue. OMB has established guidance for federal agencies on reporting, reducing, and recovering improper payments[11] and has established various work groups responsible for developing recommendations aimed at improving federal financial management activities related to reducing improper payments.

## HHS's Foster Care Program

Each year, hundreds of thousands of our nation's most vulnerable children are removed from their homes and placed in foster care, often because of abuse or neglect. While states are primarily responsible for providing safe and stable out-of-home care for these children until they are returned safely home, placed with adoptive families, or placed in other arrangements, Title IV-E of the Social Security Act provides states some federal financial support in this area.[12] ACF under HHS is responsible for administering this program and overseeing Title IV-E funds. HHS's reported fiscal year 2010 outlays to states for their Foster Care programs under Title IV-E totaled more than $4.5 billion, serving over 408,000 children, as of September 30, 2010, the most recent data available at the time of our study.

Past work by the HHS Office of Inspector General (OIG), GAO, and others have identified numerous deficiencies in state claims associated with the Title IV-E Foster Care program. In particular, the HHS OIG found hundreds of millions of dollars in unallowable claims associated with Title IV-E funding.[13] A 2006 GAO report also found variations in costs states claimed under the Title IV-E program and recommended a number of actions HHS should take to better safeguard federal resources.[14] In addition, annual state-level audits have identified weaknesses in states' use of federal funds, such as spending on unallowed activities or costs and inadequate state monitoring of federal funding.[15]

As required under IPIA, as amended, HHS has identified the Foster Care program as susceptible to significant improper payments, and has reported annually on estimated improper payment amounts for the program since 2005.[16] For fiscal year 2010, HHS reported estimated improper payments for Foster Care of about $73 million. The reported estimate slightly decreased to about $72 million for fiscal year 2011.

# OMB and Agencies Reported Progress in Estimating and Reducing Improper Payments

Federal agencies reported improper payment estimates totaling $115.3 billion in fiscal year 2011, a decrease of $5.3 billion from the revised prior year reported estimate of $120.6 billion.[17] Based on the agencies' estimates, OMB estimated that improper payments comprised about 4.7 percent of the

$2.5 trillion in fiscal year 2011 total spending for the agencies' related programs (i.e., a 4.7 percent error rate). The decrease in the fiscal year 2011 estimate—when compared to fiscal year 2010—is attributed primarily to decreases in program outlays for the Department of Labor's (Labor) Unemployment Insurance program, and decreases in reported error rates for fiscal year 2011 for the Department of the Treasury's (Treasury) Earned Income Tax Credit program, and HHS's Medicare Advantage program.

According to OMB, the $115.3 billion in estimated federal improper payments reported for fiscal year 2011 was attributable to 79 programs spread among 17 agencies. Ten of these 79 programs account for most of the $115.3 billion of reported improper payments. Specifically, these 10 programs accounted for about $107 billion or 93 percent of the total estimated improper payments agencies reported for fiscal year 2011. Table 1 shows the reported improper payment estimates and the reported primary cause(s) for the estimated improper payments for these 10 programs.

**Table 1. Improper Payment Dollar Estimates: 10 Programs with the Highest Reported Amounts in Fiscal Year 2011**

| Reported improper payment estimates | | | | |
|---|---|---|---|---|
| **Program** | **Agency** | **Dollars (in billions)** | **Error rate (percentages)** | **Reported primary cause(s)** |
| Medicare Fee-for-Service | Department of Health and Human Services | $28.8 | 8.6 | Medically unnecessary services and insufficient documentation |
| Medicaid | Department of Health and Human Services | 21.9 | 8.1 | Ineligible or indeterminable eligibility status for Medicaid beneficiaries |
| Earned Income Tax Credit | Department of the Treasury | 15.2 | 23.5 | Complexity of the tax law, structureof the program, confusion among eligible claimants, high turnover of eligible claimants, and unscrupulous return preparers |

**Table 1. (Continued)**

| Reported improper payment estimates | | | | |
|---|---|---|---|---|
| **Program** | **Agency** | **Dollars (in billions)** | **Error rate (percentages)** | **Reported primary cause(s)** |
| Unemployment Insurance | Department of Labor | 13.7 | 12.0 | Overpayment to claimants who continue to claim benefits after they return to work, ineligibility, and claimants who failed to meet active work search requirements |
| Medicare Advantage | Department of Health and Human Services | 12.4 | 11.0 | Insufficient documentation, errors in the transfer and interpretation of data, and payment calculations |
| Supplemental Security Income | Social Security Administration | 4.6 | 9.1 | Recipients failed to provide accurate and timely reports of new or increased wages |
| Old Age Survivors' and Disability Insurance | Social Security Administration | 4.5 | 0.6 | Computation errors, eligibility errors, non-verification of earnings, and incorrect processing of applications or payments |
| Supplemental Nutrition Assistance | Department of Agriculture | 2.5 | 3.8 | Incomplete or inaccurate reporting of income by participant and incorrect eligibility determination by caseworkers |
| National School Lunch | Department of Agriculture | 1.7 | 16.0 | Verification errors related to benefit calculation error, duplicate payments, insufficient documentation, and fraud or misrepresentation by program participants or others |
| Medicare Prescription Drug Benefit | Department of Health and Human Services | 1.7 | 3.2 | Payment errors, payment adjustment errors, and complexity of program |

Source: GAO analysis of agencies' PARs and AFRs for fiscal year 2011.

## Table 2. Improper Payment Error Rates: 10 Programs with the Highest Reported Rates in Fiscal Year 2011

| Reported improper payment estimates | | | | |
|---|---|---|---|---|
| **Program** | **Agency** | **Error rate (percentages)** | **Dollars (in millions)** | **Reported primary cause(s)** |
| Disaster Assistance Loans | Small Business Administration | 28.4% | $96.3 | Loan documentation errors |
| School Breakfast | Department of Agriculture | 25.0% | $705.0 | Authentication and administrative errors, including authentic-cating the accuracy of qualifying for program specific requirements, criteria, or conditions |
| Earned Income Tax Credit | Department of the Treasury | 23.5% | $15,200.0 | Complexity of the tax law, structure of the program, confusion among eligible claimants, high turnover of eligible claimants, and unscrupulous return preparers |
| National School Lunch | Department of Agriculture | 16.0% | $1,716.0 | Verification errors related to benefit calculation error, duplicate payments, insufficient documentation, and fraud or misrepresent-tation by program participants or others |
| State Home Per Diem Grants | Department of Veterans Affairs | 13.7% | $97.6 | Documentation and administrative errors related to ineligible recipients, noncompliance with policies and procedures, incorrect amounts, ineligible goods, and lack of documentation |

**Table 2. (Continued)**

| Reported improper payment estimates | | | | |
|---|---|---|---|---|
| **Program** | **Agency** | **Error rate (percentages)** | **Dollars (in millions)** | **Reported primary cause(s)** |
| Supplies and Materials | Department of Veterans Affairs | 13.6% | $221.1 | Documentation and administrative errors related to noncompliance with policies and procedures, lack of documentation, ineligible goods, incorrect amounts, and discounts not taken |
| Non-VA Care Fee | Department of Veterans Affairs | 12.4% | $522.9 | Verification and documentation and administrative errors related to incorrect application of payment methodologies, lack of documentation, lack of authorization, and data entry errors |
| Unemployment Insurance | Department of Labor | 12.0% | $13,697.0 | Overpayment to claimants who continue to claim benefits after they return to work, ineligibility, and claimants who failed to meet active work search requirements |
| Child Care and Development Fund | Department of Health and Human Services | 11.2% | $638.0 | Documentation and administrative errors caused by missing or insufficient documentation |
| Medicare Advantage | Department of Health and Human Services | 1<br>1.0% | $12,390.0 | Insufficient documentation, errors in the transfer and interpretation of data, and payment calculation errors |

Source: GAO analysis of agencies' PARs and AFRs for fiscal year 2011.

While the programs identified in the table above represented the largest dollar amounts of improper payments, 4 of these programs also had some of the highest program improper payment error rates.[18] As shown in table 2, the 10 programs with the highest error rates accounted for $45 billion, or 39 percent of the total estimated improper payments, and had rates ranging from 11.0 percent to 28.4 percent for fiscal year 2011.

Since the implementation of IPIA in 2004, federal agencies have worked to identify new programs or activities as risk-susceptible and report estimated improper payment amounts. The fiscal year 2011 governmentwide estimate of $115.3 billion included improper payment estimates for nine additional programs that did not report an estimate in fiscal year 2010, with the HHS Medicare Prescription Drug Benefit (Part D) program having the highest dollar estimate of the newly included programs. We view these agencies' efforts as a positive step toward increasing the transparency of the magnitude of improper payments across the federal government. However, OMB did not include three additional programs providing estimates in fiscal year 2011 in the governmentwide totals because their estimation methodologies were still under development. The three excluded programs were the Department of Education's (Education) Direct Loan, Department of Defense's (DOD) Defense Finance and Accounting Service Commercial Pay, and DOD's U.S. Army Corps of Engineers Commercial Pay.

A number of federal agencies have reported progress in reducing improper payment error rates in some of their programs and activities. For example, we identified 40 federal agency programs, or about 50 percent of the total programs reporting improper payment estimates in fiscal year 2011, that reported a reduction in the error rate of estimated improper payments in fiscal year 2011 when compared to fiscal year 2010 error rates. However, these rates have not been independently verified or audited. The following are examples of agencies that reported reductions in program error rates and estimated improper payment amounts (along with corrective actions to reduce improper payments) in their fiscal year 2011 PARs, AFRs, or annual reports.

- Treasury reported that the fiscal year 2011 Earned Income Tax Credit (EITC) program's estimated improper payment amount decreased from the fiscal year 2010 amount of $16.9 billion to $15.2 billion, which represented a decrease in the error rate from 26.3 percent to 23.5 percent. Treasury reported that corrective actions taken to reduce improper payments primarily focused on completing examinations of tax returns that claimed the EITC before issuing the EITC portion of the refund, identifying math or other statistical irregularities in taxpayer returns, and comparing income information provided by the taxpayer with matching information from employers to identify discrepancies.

- HHS reported that the fiscal year 2011 estimated improper payment amount for the Medicare Advantage (Part C) program decreased from the fiscal year 2010 reported amount of $13.6 billion to $12.4 billion, which represented a decrease in the error rate from 14.1 percent to 11.0 percent. HHS reported that it reduced payment errors by continuing to routinely implement controls in its payment system to ensure accurate and timely payments, and implementing three key initiatives—contract-level audits, physician outreach, and Medicare Advantage organization guidance and training.

In addition, agencies have further developed the use of recovery audits to recapture improper payments. In 2010, the President set goals, as part of the Accountable Government Initiative, for federal agencies to reduce overall improper payments by $50 billion, and recapture at least $2 billion in improper contract payments and overpayments to healthcare providers, by the end of fiscal year 2012. For fiscal year 2011, OMB reported that governmentwide agencies recaptured $1.25 billion in improper payments to contractors and vendors. Over half of this amount, $797 million, can be attributed to the Medicare recovery audit contractor program, which identifies improper Medicare payments—both overpayments and underpayments—in all 50 states. Cumulatively, OMB reported $1.9 billion recaptured from improper payments to contractors, vendors, and healthcare providers for fiscal years 2010 and 2011 towards the President's goal of recapturing at least $2 billion by the end of fiscal year 2012.

## Governmentwide Challenges to Estimating and Evaluating Improper Payments

Despite reported progress in reducing estimated improper payment amounts and error rates for some programs and activities during fiscal year 2011, the federal government continues to face challenges in determining the full extent of improper payments. Specifically, some agencies have not yet reported estimates for all risk-susceptible programs, and some agencies' estimating methodologies need to be refined. Until federal agencies are able to implement effective processes to completely and accurately identify the full extent of improper payments and implement appropriate corrective actions to effectively reduce improper payments, the federal government will not have reasonable assurance that the use of taxpayer funds is adequately safeguarded. In this regard, at the request of this Subcommittee, we recently completed our review of the improper payment estimation methodology used by HHS's Foster Care program. As discussed in our report released today,[19] we found that the Foster Care program's improper payment estimation methodology was deficient in all three key areas—planning, selection, and evaluation—and consequently did not result in a reasonably accurate estimate of the extent of Foster Care improper payments. Further, the validity of the reporting of reduced Foster Care program error rates was questionable, and we found that several weaknesses impaired ACF's ability to assess the effectiveness of corrective actions to reduce improper payments.

## Challenges in Developing Improper Payment Estimates

We found that not all agencies have developed improper payment estimates for all of the programs and activities they identified as susceptible to significant improper payments. Specifically, three federal entities did not report fiscal year 2011 estimated improper payment amounts for four risk-susceptible programs.[20] In one example, HHS's fiscal year 2011 reporting cited statutory limitations for its state-administered Temporary Assistance for Needy Families (TANF) program,[21] that prohibited it from requiring states to participate in developing an improper payment estimate for the TANF program. Despite these limitations, HHS officials stated that they will continue to work with states and explore options to allow for future estimates for the program. For fiscal year 2011, the TANF program reported outlays of about $17 billion. For another program, HHS cited the Children's Health Insurance Program Reauthorization Act of 2009[22] as prohibiting HHS from calculating or publishing any national or state-specific payment error rates for the Children's Health Insurance Program (CHIP) until 6 months after the new payment error rate measurement rule became effective on September 10, 2010. According to its fiscal year 2011 agency financial report, HHS plans to report estimated improper payment amounts for CHIP in fiscal year 2012. For fiscal year 2011, HHS reported federal outlays of about $9 billion for CHIP.

As previously mentioned, OMB excluded estimated improper payment amounts for two DOD programs from the governmentwide total because those programs were still developing their estimating methodologies—Defense Finance and Accounting Service (DFAS) Commercial Pay,[23] with fiscal year 2011 outlays of $368.5 billion, and U.S. Army Corps of Engineers

Commercial Pay, with fiscal year 2011 outlays of $30.5 billion. In DOD's fiscal year 2011 agency financial report, DOD reported that improper payment estimates for these programs were based on improper payments detected through various pre-payment and post-payment review processes rather than using methodologies similar to those used for DOD's other programs, including statistically valid random sampling or reviewing 100 percent of payments.

Both GAO[24] and the DOD Inspector General (IG)[25] have previously reported on weaknesses in DOD's payment controls, including weaknesses in its process for assessing the risk of improper payments and reporting estimated amounts. DOD's payment controls are hindered by inadequate payment processing controls, poor financial systems, and inadequate supporting documentation. The DOD IG reported in March 2011 that deficiencies in a key component of this process could lead to erroneously categorizing a high percentage of potential improper payments as proper.[26] Further, the DOD IG reported that DOD's risk of making improper payments was high and identified deficiencies in DOD's estimate of high-dollar overpayments that caused it to underreport its improper payments.[27] Until DOD fully and effectively implements a statistically valid estimating process for its commercial payments and addresses the known control deficiencies in its commercial payment processes, the governmentwide improper payment estimates will continue to be incomplete. We are currently working on an engagement related to improper payment reporting at DOD.

For fiscal year 2011, two agency auditors reported on compliance issues with IPIA and IPERA as part of their 2011 financial statement audits. Specifically, the Department of Agriculture (USDA) auditors identified noncompliance with the requirements of IPERA regarding the design of program internal controls related to improper payments. In the other noncompliance issue, while for fiscal year 2011 HHS estimated an annual amount of improper payments for some of its risk-susceptible programs, a key requirement of IPIA, it did not report an improper payment estimate for its TANF program and CHIP. Fiscal year 2011 marked the eighth consecutive year that auditors for HHS reported noncompliance issues with IPIA.

We recognize that measuring improper payments for federal programs and designing and implementing actions to reduce or eliminate them are not simple tasks, particularly for grant programs that rely on administration efforts at the state level. The estimation methodologies for these types of programs may vary considerably because of differences in program designs across the states. For example, as I will discuss in more detail later in this statement, the Foster

Care program leveraged an existing process to estimate improper payments that included a review of a child's eligibility for Title IV-E federal funding as claimed by the states administering the program. In another example, the improper payment estimate for HHS's Medicaid program is based on the results of three different reviews—eligibility, fee-for-service, and managed care—of claims payments made by states to health care providers. The fee-for-service and managed care reviews both include a data processing review to validate that claims were processed correctly. The fee-for-service review also includes a medical necessity determination. The eligibility review identifies payments made for services to beneficiaries that were improperly paid because of erroneous eligibility decisions. We are currently working on an engagement related to improper payment reporting for the Medicaid program. Because of these state differences and complexities within programs, as we previously reported,[28] communication, coordination, and cooperation among federal agencies and the states will be critical to effectively estimate national improper payment rates and meet IPIA reporting requirements for state-administered programs.

## Case Study: Foster Care Program Faces Challenges in Estimating Improper Payments and Evaluating Corrective Actions

The results of our recently completed study of the improper payment estimation methodology used by HHS's Foster Care program serve to provide a more detailed perspective on the challenges one federal agency faced in attempting to develop a complete and accurate nationwide estimate for a program largely administered at the state level. Further, this case study provides an example of the types of problems that may exist but go undetected because of the lack of independent assessments of the reported information. As we previously testified before this Subcommittee,[29] separate assessments conducted by agency auditors provide a valuable independent validation of agencies' efforts to report reliable information under IPIA. Independent assessments can also enhance an agency's ability to identify sound performance measures, monitor progress against those measures, and help establish performance and results expectations. Without this type of validation or other types of reviews performed by GAO or agency OIGs, it is difficult to reliably determine the full magnitude of deficiencies that may exist governmentwide in agencies' IPIA implementation efforts. For example, our case study of the Foster Care program found that although ACF had established a process to calculate a national improper payment estimate, the estimate was not based on a statistically valid methodology and consequently did not reflect a reasonably accurate estimate of the extent of Foster Care improper payments. Further, without accurate data, the validity of the Foster Care program's reported reductions in improper payments was questionable, and ACF's ability to reliably assess the effectiveness of its corrective actions was impaired.

### *Deficiencies in Foster Care's Estimation Methodology*

For programs administered at the state level such as Foster Care, OMB guidance provides that statistically valid annual estimates of improper payments may be based on either data for all states or on statistical data from a sample to generate a national dollar estimate and improper payment rate. In this case, ACF took its existing Title IV-E Foster Care program eligibility review process, already in place under the Social Security Act, and also used it for IPIA estimation. ACF provides a national estimated error rate based on a rolling average of error rates identified in states examined on a 3-year cycle. As a result, ACF's IPIA reporting for each year is based on new data for about one-third of the states and previous years' data for the remaining two-thirds of the states. To calculate a national estimate of improper payments, ACF uses error rates that span a 3-year period of Title IV-E eligibility reviews in the 50 states, the District of Columbia, and Puerto Rico. ACF applies the percentage dollar error rate from the sample to the total payments for the period under review for each state.

ACF's methodology for estimating Foster Care improper payments was approved by OMB in 2004 with the understanding that continuing efforts would be taken to improve the accuracy of ACF's estimates of improper payments in the ensuing years. ACF, however, has since continued to generally follow its initial 2004 methodology. When compared to federal statistical guidance and internal control standards, we found it to be deficient in all three phases of its fiscal year 2010 estimation methodology—planning, selection, and evaluation—as summarized in table 3. These deficiencies impaired the accuracy and completeness of the Foster Care program improper payment estimate of $73 million reported for fiscal year 2010.

**Planning.** ACF's annual IPIA reporting for the Foster Care program did not include about two-thirds of program expenditures, as shown in figure 1. Specifically, the estimate included improper payments for only one type of program payment activity—maintenance payments—which, for fiscal year 2010, represented 34 percent of the total federal share of expenditures for the Foster Care program. Administrative and other payments, such as those related to the operation and development of the Statewide Automated Child Welfare Information System (SACWIS), were not considered in ACF's IPIA estimation process and thus were not included in the Foster Care program improper payment estimate. OMB's December 2004 approval of ACF's proposed methodology included an expectation that ACF would develop a plan and timetable to test administrative expenses by April 2005. ACF has conducted various pilots in this area since 2007 with the goal of ensuring that improper payment data for administrative costs are sufficiently reliable and valid without imposing undue burden on states. Although ACF expects to estimate for administrative improper payments and recognizes the importance of doing so, it has not yet taken action to augment its existing methodology.

**Table 3. Deficiencies in ACF's Methodology to Estimate Foster Care Improper Payments**

| Estimation methodology phase | Deficiencies by phase |
|---|---|
| Planning | • Methodology islimited to identifying improper payments for only one-third of the total federal share of foster care expenditures—maintenance payments.<br>• The case-level population data used to derive the foster care improper payment estimate does not contain the associated payment data needed for a direct estimate of the paymenterror rate and the total amount of dollars that were improperly paid. |
| Selection | • ACF has not established up-front data quality procedures over the case-level population data, self-reported by states, prior to sample selection.<br>• Sample selection process includes a high percentage of replacement cases due to inaccurate information contained in the case-level population data. |
| Evaluation | • Methodology does not include procedures on how to identify payment errors related to underpayments and duplicate payments during the review of sampled cases across states.<br>• Methodology used to aggregate state-level improper payment data does not take into account each state's margin of error, which is needed to calculate an overall program improper payment estimate with a 90 percent confidence level generally required by OMB guidance. |

Source: GAO analysis of ACF's methodology to estimate Foster Care improper payments.

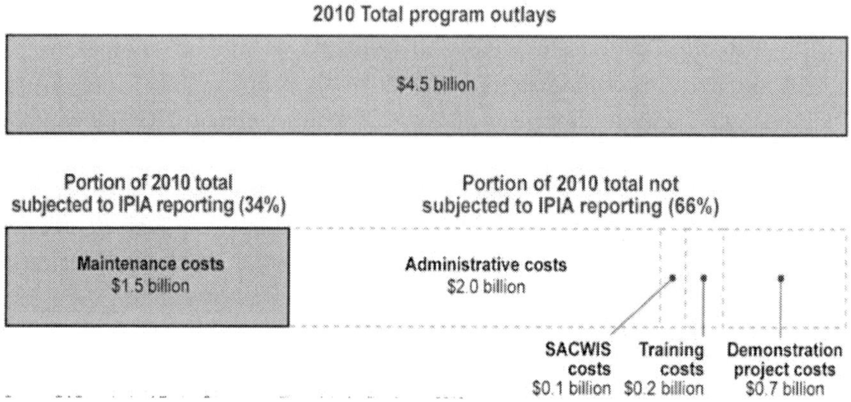


Source: GAO analysis of ACF's methodology to estimate Foster Care improper payments.

Figure 1. Foster Care Program Outlays for Fiscal Year 2010 Covered under IPIA Reporting.

**Selection.** The population of data from which ACF selected its sample—the Adoption and Foster Care Analysis and Reporting System (AFCARS)[30]—were not reliable because ACF's sampling methodology did not provide for up-front data quality control procedures to (1) ensure that the population of cases was complete prior to its sample selection and (2) identify inaccuracies in the data field used for sample selection. Specifically, ACF had to replace a high percentage of cases sampled from the database of Foster Care cases for the fiscal year 2010 reporting period because of inaccurate information in AFCARS.

- Of the original 4,570 sample cases ACF selected for testing in its primary and secondary reviews for fiscal year 2010, 298 cases (almost 7 percent) had to be replaced with substitutes because the selected cases had not received Title IV-E Foster Care maintenance payments during the period under review.
- Of the 298 over-sampled cases used to replace the cases initially selected, 63 cases (more than 21 percent) then had to be replaced again because those cases had also not received Title IV-E Foster Care maintenance payments during the period under review.
- Further, although we were able to determine how many sampled (or over-sampled) cases had to be replaced because available records showed no Title IV-E payment was received during the reporting

period, neither GAO nor ACF were able to determine the extent to which the opposite occurred—cases that had received a payment (and therefore should have been included in the sample population) had not been coded as receiving Title IV-E payments.

Without developing a statistically valid sampling methodology that incorporates up-front data quality controls to ensure complete and accurate information on the population, including payment data, ACF cannot provide assurance that its reported improper payment estimate accurately and completely represents the extent of improper maintenance payments in the Foster Care program.

**Evaluation.** Although ACF's methodology identified some errors related to underpayments and duplicate or excessive payments, it did not include procedures to reliably determine the full extent of such errors. In its fiscal year 2010 agency financial report, ACF reported that underpayments and duplicate or excessive payments represented 19 percent and 6 percent, respectively, or 25 percent of the errors that caused improper payments.[31] However, the extent of underpayments and duplicate or excessive payment errors identified varied widely by state, and in some instances were not identified at all. For example, ACF did not identify underpayments in 31 of 51 state eligibility reviews and did not identify duplicate or excessive payments in 36 of 51 state eligibility reviews.[32] We did not assess the validity of the reported data. However, the absence of such errors for some states seems inconsistent with the general distribution of errors reported elsewhere. Further, the lack of detailed procedures for identifying any such payment errors may have contributed to the variation or to whether the teams found any errors. The purpose of the eligibility reviews is to validate the accuracy of a state's claim for reimbursement of payments made on behalf of eligible children or the accuracy of federal financial assistance provided to states. Without detailed procedures to guide review teams in the identification of underpayments and duplicate or excessive payments, ACF cannot provide assurance that it has identified the full extent of any such errors in its Foster Care program.

### *Validity of Reported Foster Care Program Improper Payment Reductions Is Questionable*

The weaknesses we identified in ACF's methodology to estimate improper payments in the Foster Care program also impaired its ability to reliably assess the extent to which its corrective actions reduced Foster Care program improper payments. For example, although ACF has reported significantly reduced estimated improper maintenance payments, from a baseline error rate of 10.33 percent for 2004 to a 4.9 percent error rate for 2010, the validity of ACF's reporting of reduced improper payment error rates is questionable because the previously discussed weaknesses in its estimation methodology impaired the accuracy and completeness of the reported estimate and error rate. In addition, we found that ACF's ability to reliably assess the extent to which its corrective actions reduced improper payments was impaired by weaknesses in its requirements for state-level corrective actions. For example, ACF used the number of cases found in error rather than the dollar amount of improper payments identified to determine whether a state was required to implement corrective actions. ACF required states to implement corrective actions through a program improvement plan, if during the Title IV-E primary eligibility review, a state was found to have an error rate exceeding 5 percent of the number of cases reviewed. We identified six states that were found substantially compliant in their primary eligibility reviews as their case error rates were below the established 5 percent threshold. However, the dollar-based improper payment rates for those six states ranged from 5.1 percent to 19.8 percent—based on the percentage of improper payment dollars found in the sample. Because dollar-based improper payment rates are not used in applying the corrective action strategy, ACF's method cannot effectively measure states' progress over time in reducing improper payments. It also cannot effectively help determine whether further action is needed to minimize future improper payments. This limits the extent to which states are held accountable for the reduction of improper payments in the Foster Care program.

Our report released today includes seven recommendations to help improve ACF's methodology for estimating improper payments for the Foster Care program and its corrective action process.[33] In commenting on our draft report, HHS agreed that its improper payment estimation efforts can and should be improved, generally concurred with four of our recommendations, and agreed to continue to study the remaining three recommendations. We reaffirm the need for all seven recommendations.

## Current and Possible Strategies to Move Forward in Reducing Improper Payments

A number of actions are under way across the federal government to help advance improper payment reduction goals. Completing these initiatives, as well as designing and implementing enhanced strategies in the future, will be needed to effectively reduce the federal government's improper payments. Identifying and analyzing the root causes of improper payments is key to developing effective corrective actions and implementing the controls needed to reduce and prevent improper payments. In this regard, implementing strong preventive controls are particularly important as these controls can serve as the front-line defense against improper payments. Proactively preventing improper payments increases public confidence in the administration of benefit programs and avoids the difficulties associated with the "pay and chase"[34] aspects of recovering improper payments. For example, addressing program design issues that are a factor in causing improper payments may be an effective preventive strategy. Effective monitoring and reporting will also be important to help detect any emerging improper payment issues. In addition, agencies' actions to enhance detective controls to identify and recover overpayments could help increase the attention to preventing, identifying, and recovering improper payments. For instance, agency strategies to enhance incentives for grantees, such as state and local governments, will be important.

### Identifying and Analyzing Root Causes of Improper Payments

Agencies cited a number of causes for the estimated $115.3 billion in reported improper payments, including insufficient documentation; incorrect computations; changes in program requirements; and, in some cases, fraud. Beginning in fiscal year 2011, according to OMB's guidance,[35] agencies were required to classify the root causes of estimated improper payments into three general categories for reporting purposes: (1) documentation and administrative errors, (2) authentication and medical necessity errors, and (3) verification errors.[36] Reliable information on the root causes of the current improper payment estimates is necessary for agencies to target effective corrective actions and implement preventive measures.

While agencies generally reported some description of the causes of improper payments for their respective programs in their fiscal year 2011 reports, many agencies did not use the three categories prescribed by OMB to classify the types of errors and quantify how many errors can be attributed to that category. Of the 79 programs with improper payment estimates in fiscal year 2011, we found that agencies reported the root cause information using the required categories for 42 programs in their fiscal year 2011 PARs and AFRs. Together, these programs represented about $46 billion, or 40 percent of the total reported $115.3 billion in improper payment estimates for fiscal year 2011. Of the $46 billion, the estimated improper payments amounts were spread across the three categories, with documentation and administrative errors being cited most often. We could not calculate the dollar amounts associated with each category because the narratives included in some of the agencies' reporting of identified causes were not sufficiently detailed or documented. Thorough and properly documented analysis regarding the root causes is critical if federal agencies are to effectively identify and implement corrective and preventive actions across their various programs.

## Implementing Effective Preventive Controls to Avoid Improper Payments

Many agencies and programs are in the process of implementing preventive controls to avoid improper payments, including overpayments and underpayments. Preventive controls may involve a variety of activities, such as up-front validation of eligibility, predictive analytic tests, training programs, and timely resolution of audit findings, as described below. Further, addressing program design deficiencies that have caused improper payments may be considered as part of an effective preventive strategy.

- **Up-front eligibility validation through data sharing.** Data sharing allows entities that make payments—to contractors, vendors, participants in benefit programs, and others—to compare information from different sources to help ensure that payments are appropriate. When effectively implemented, data sharing can be particularly useful in confirming initial or continuing eligibility of participants in benefit programs and in identifying any improper payments that have already been made. Also, in June 2010, the President issued a presidential memorandum, titled *Enhancing Payment Accuracy Through a "Do Not Pay List"*, to help prevent improper payments to ineligible recipients.[37] This memorandum also directs agencies to review prepayment and reward procedures and ensure that a thorough review of available databases with relevant information on eligibility occurs before the release of any federal funds. Analyses and reporting on the extent to which agencies are participating in data sharing activities, and additional data sharing efforts that agencies are currently pursuing or would like to pursue, are other important elements that merit consideration as part of future strategies to advance the federal government's efforts to reduce improper payments.

For example, Labor reported that its Unemployment Insurance program utilizes HHS's National Directory of New Hires database[38] to improve the ability to detect overpayments caused by individuals who claim benefits after returning to work—the largest single cause of overpayments reported in the program. In June 2011, Labor established the mandatory use of the database for state benefit payment control no later than December 2011. Labor also recommended operating procedures for cross-matching activity for national and state directories of new hires.

In another case, to address the issue of inaccuracy of self-reported financial income on applications for student aid, Education, in conjunction with the Internal Revenue Service (IRS), implemented a 6-month pilot version of an IRS data retrieval tool in January 2010 for its Pell Grant Program. The tool allows student aid applicants or their parents to transfer certain tax return information from IRS directly to Education's online application. Education reported that nearly 3.5 million students used the data exchange tool, representing approximately 21 percent of the applications submitted for the 2011-2012 academic year.

- **Predictive analytic technologies.** In ongoing work, GAO is assessing HHS's Centers for Medicare and Medicaid Services' (CMS) use of technologies that are intended to support the agency's efforts to prevent payment of fraudulent claims. The Small Business Jobs Act of 2010 requires CMS to use predictive modeling and other analytic techniques—known as predictive analytic technologies—both to identify and to prevent improper payments under the Medicare Fee-for-Service program.[39] These predictive analytic technologies are to be used to analyze and identify Medicare provider networks, billing patterns, and beneficiary utilization patterns and detect those that represent a high risk of fraudulent activity. Through such analysis, CMS expects to more effectively identify unusual or suspicious patterns or abnormalities that may provide information that could be useful in prioritizing additional review of suspicious transactions before payment is made. The 2010 act required that CMS's program integrity analysts and contractors begin using these technologies on July 1, 2011, in the 10 states identified by CMS as having the highest risk of fraud, waste, or abuse in Medicare Fee-for-Service payments. CMS began using these technologies, available through CMS's new Fraud Prevention System, to screen all Fee-for-Service claims nationwide prior to payment as of June 30, 2011.

- **Training programs for providers, staff, and beneficiaries.** Training can be a key element in any effort to prevent improper payments from occurring. This can include both training staff on how to prevent and detect improper payments and training providers or beneficiaries on program requirements. For example, the Medicaid Integrity Institute, an initiative of CMS's Medicaid Integrity Group (MIG), trains state-level staff and facilitates networking by sponsoring free workshops for states. In addition, the MIG sponsors education programs for beneficiaries and providers, such as pharmacy providers, to promote best prescribing practices and appropriate prescribing guidelines based on Food and Drug Administration labeling, potentially reducing improper payments.[40]
- **Timely resolution of audit findings.** *Standards for Internal Control in the Federal Government*[41] requires that the findings of audits and other reviews be promptly resolved. Managers are to (1) evaluate findings from audits and other reviews promptly, including those showing deficiencies and recommendations reported by auditors and others who evaluate agencies' operations; (2) determine proper actions in response to findings and recommendations from audits and reviews; and (3) complete, within established time frames, all actions that correct or otherwise resolve the matters brought to management's attention.
- **Program design review and refinement.** To the extent that provider enrollment and eligibility verification problems are identified as a significant root cause in a specific program, agencies may look to establish enhanced controls in this area. For example, CMS has taken steps to strengthen standards and procedures for Medicare provider enrollment to help reduce the risk of providers intent on defrauding or abusing the program.[42] Further, exploring whether certain complex program requirements, inconsistent program requirements, or both,

such as eligibility criteria and requirements for provider enrollment, contribute to improper payments could be used to lend insight to developing effective strategies for enhancing compliance and in identifying opportunities for streamlining or changing the e igi bility or other program control requirements.

## Implementing Effective Detective Controls to Identify and Recover Overpayments

Although strong preventive controls remain the frontline defense against improper payments, agencies' improper payment reduction strategies could also consider actions to establish additional effective detection techniques to quickly identify and recover those improper payments that do occur. Detection activities play a significant role not only in identifying improper payments, but also in providing data on why these payments were made and, in turn, highlighting areas that could benefit from strengthened prevention controls. The following are examples of key detection activities to be considered.

- **Data mining.** Data mining is a computer-based control activity that analyzes diverse data for relationships that have not previously been discovered. The central repository of data commonly used to perform data mining is called a data warehouse. Data warehouses store tables of historical and current information that are logically grouped. As a tool in detecting improper payments, data mining of a data warehouse can enable an organization to efficiently identify potential improper payments, such as multiple payments for an individual invoice to an individual recipient on the same date, or to the same address. For example, in the Medicare and Medicaid program, data on claims are stored in geographically disbursed systems and databases that are not readily available to CMS's program integrity analysts. Over the past decade, CMS has been working to consolidate program integrity data and analytical tools for detecting fraud, waste, and abuse. The agency's efforts led to the initiation of the Integrated Data Repository (IDR) program, which is intended to provide CMS and its program integrity contractors with a centralized source that contains Medicaid and Medicare data from the many disparate and dispersed legacy systems and databases. CMS subsequently developed the One Program Integrity (One PI) program,[43] a web-based portal and set of analytical tools by which these data can be accessed and analyzed to help identify any cases of fraudulent, wasteful, and abusive payments based on patterns of paid claims.[44]

- **Recovery auditing.** While internal control should be maintained to help prevent improper payments, recovery auditing could be included as a part of agencies' strategy for identifying and recovering contractor overpayments. The Tax Relief and Health Care Act of 2006 required CMS to implement a national Medicare recovery audit contractor (RAC) program by January 1, 2010.[45] In fiscal year 2011, HHS reported that the Medicare Fee-for-Service recovery audit program identified $961 million in overpayments and recovered $797 million nationwide. Further, the Medicaid RAC program was established by the Patient Protection and Affordable Care Act.[46] Under this program, each state is to contract with a RAC to identify and recover Medicaid overpayments and identify any underpayments. The final regulations provided that state Medicaid RACs were to be implemented by January 1, 2012. Similar to the Medicare RACs, Medicaid RACs will be paid on a contingency fee basis—a percentage of any recovered overpayments plus incentive payments for the detection of underpayments.

  It is important to note that some agencies have reported statutory or regulatory barriers that affect their ability to pursue recovery auditing. For example, in fiscal year 2011, the Office of Personnel Management (OPM) reported that it faces regulatory barriers that restrict its ability to recover improper payments for its Retirement Program. OPM reported that based on current law and Treasury's regulations, financial institutions are barred from providing OPM with the information necessary to recover various improper payments. Only the Social Security Administration, Railroad Retirement Board, and the Department of Veterans Affairs have been authorized to receive the information necessary to identify the withdrawer to attempt to recover any improper payments. According to OPM, Treasury has drafted language to address the issue and is working to publish a notice of proposed rule making to amend its regulation.

  In another instance, USDA reported that Section 281 of the Department of Agriculture Reorganization Act of 1994[47] precluded the use of recovery auditing techniques because Section 281 provides that 90 days after the decision of a state, county, or an area committee is final, no action may be taken to recover the amounts found to have been erroneously disbursed as a result of the decision unless the participant had reason to believe that the decision was erroneous. This statute is commonly referred to as the Finality Rule. As part of its annual improper payments reporting, USDA did not cite an alternative approach for implementing a recovery auditing strategy.

- **Federal-state incentives.** Another area for further exploration for agencies' improper payment reduction strategies is the broader use of incentives for states to implement effective detective controls.[48] Agencies have applied limited incentives and penalties for encouraging improved state administration to reduce improper payments. Incentives and penalties can be helpful to create management reform and to ensure adherence to performance standards.

Chairman Carper, Ranking Member Brown, and Members of the Subcommittee, this completes my prepared statement. I would be pleased to respond to any questions that you may have at this time.

## RELATED GAO PRODUCTS

*Foster Care Program: Improved Processes Needed to Estimate Improper Payments and Evaluate Related Corrective Actions*. GAO. Washington, D.C.: March 7, 2012.

*Improper Payments: Moving Forward with Governmentwide Reduction Strategies*. GAO. Washington, D.C.: February 7, 2012.

For our report on the U.S. government's consolidated financial statements for fiscal year 2011, see Department of the Treasury. *2011 Financial Report of the United States Government*. Washington, D.C.:December 23, 2011, pp. 211-231.

*Medicaid Program Integrity: Expanded Federal Role Presents Challenges to and Opportunities for Assisting States*. GAO. Washington, D.C.: December 7, 2011.

*DOD Financial Management: Weaknesses in Controls over the Use of Public Funds and Related Improper Payments*. GAO. Washington, D.C.: September 22, 2011.

*Improper Payments: Reported Medicare Estimates and Key Remediation Strategies*. GAO. Washington, D.C.: July 28, 2011.

*Fraud Detection Systems: Centers for Medicare and Medicaid Services Needs to Ensure More Widespread Use*. GAO. Washington, D.C.: June 30, 2011.

*Improper Payments: Recent Efforts to Address Improper Payments and Remaining Challenges*. GAO. Washington, D.C.: April 15, 2011.

*Status of Fiscal Year 2010 Federal Improper Payments Reporting*. GAO. Washington, D.C.: March 25, 2011.

*Opportunities to Reduce Potential Duplication in Government Programs, Save Tax Dollars, and Enhance Revenue*. GAO. Washington, D.C.: March 1, 2011.

*High-Risk Series: An Update*. GAO. Washington, D.C.: February 2011.

*Improper Payments: Significant Improvements Needed in DOD's Efforts to Address Improper Payment and Recovery Auditing Requirements*. GAO. Washington, D.C.: July 29, 2009.

*Improper Payments: Progress Made but Challenges Remain in Estimating and Reducing Improper Payments*. GAO. Washington, D.C.: April 22, 2009.

*Improper Payments: Status of Agencies' Efforts to Address Improper Payment and Recovery Auditing Requirements*. GAO. Washington, D.C.: January 31, 2008.

*Improper Payments: Federal Executive Branch Agencies' Fiscal Year 2007 Improper Payment Estimate Reporting*. GAO. Washington, D.C.: January 23, 2008.

*Improper Payments: Weaknesses in USAID's and NASA's Implementation of the Improper Payments Information Act and Recovery Auditing*. GAO. Washington, D.C.: November 9, 2007.

*Improper Payments: Agencies' Efforts to Address Improper Payment and Recovery Auditing Requirements Continue*. GAO. Washington, D.C.: March 29, 2007.

*Improper Payments: Incomplete Reporting under the Improper Payments Information Act Masks the Extent of the Problem*. GAO. Washington, D.C.: December 5, 2006.

*Improper Payments: Agencies' Fiscal Year 2005 Reporting under the Improper Payments Information Act Remains Incomplete*. GAO. Washington, D.C.: November 14, 2006.

*Improper Payments: Federal and State Coordination Needed to Report National Improper Payment Estimates on Federal Programs*. GAO. Washington, D.C.: April 14, 2006.

## End Notes

[1] It is important to recognize that improper payment estimates reported by federal agencies in fiscal year 2011 are not intended to be an estimate of fraud in federal agencies' programs and activities. An improper payment is defined as any payment that should not have been made or that was made in an incorrect amount (including overpayments and underpayments) under statutory, contractual, administrative, or other legally applicable requirements. It includes any payment to an ineligible recipient, any payment for an ineligible good or service, any duplicate payment, payment for a good or service not received (except for such payments where authorized by law), and any payment that does not account for credit for applicable discounts. Office of Management and Budget guidance also instructs agencies to report as improper payments any payments for which insufficient or no documentation was found.

[2] See the Related GAO Products list at the end of this statement for a selection of the products related to these issues.

[3] GAO, *Foster Care Program: Improved Processes Needed to Estimate Improper Payments and Evaluate Related Corrective Actions*, GAO-12-312 (Washington, D.C.:Mar. 7, 2012).

[4] GAO.

[5] Department of the Treasury, *2011 Financial Report of the United States Government* (Washington, D.C.: Dec. 23, 2011), 211-231.

[6] GAO.

[7] Pub. L. No. 107-300, 116 Stat. 2350 (Nov. 26, 2002).

[8] Pub. L. No. 111-204, 124 Stat. 2224 (July 22, 2010).

[9] IPERA defines "significant improper payments" as gross annual improper payments in the program exceeding (1) both 2.5 percent of program outlays and $10 million of all program or activity payments during the fiscal year reported or (2) $100 million (regardless of the improper payment error rate). Further, the threshold for "significant improper payments" will be reduced for fiscal year 2014 and each year thereafter to gross annual improper payments in the program exceeding (1) both 1.5 percent of program outlays and $10 million of all program or activity payments during the fiscal year reported or (2) $100 million (regardless of the improper payment error rate).

[10] Section 831 of the National Defense Authorization Act for Fiscal Year 2002, Pub. L. No. 107-107, div. A, 115 Stat. 1012, 1186 (Dec. 28, 2001), required that agencies that enter into contracts with a total value in excess of $500 million in a fiscal year carry out a cost-effective program for identifying and recovering amounts erroneously paid to contractors. IPERA repealed these requirements.

[11] OMB Circular No. A-136 Revised, *Financial Reporting Requirements* (Oct. 27, 2011); OMB Memorandum M-11-16, *Issuance of Revised Parts I and II to Appendix C of OMB Circular A-123* (Apr. 14, 2011); OMB Memorandum M-11-04, *Increasing Efforts to Recapture Improper Payments by Intensifying and Expanding Payment Recapture Audits* (Nov. 16, 2010); and OMB Memorandum M-10-13, *Issuance of Part III to OMB Circular A-123, Appendix. C* (Mar. 22, 2010).

[12] Codified, as amended, at 42 U.S.C. §§ 670-679c.

[13] Examples of HHS OIG reports include the following: HHS OIG, *Audit of Allegheny County Title IV-E Foster Care Claims From October 1997 Through September 2002*, A-03-08-00554 (Jan. 4, 2011); *Review of Title IV-E Foster Care Costs Claimed on Behalf of Delinquent Children in Georgia*, A-04-07-03519 (June 17, 2010); *Review of California's Title IV-E Claims for Payments Made by Los Angeles County to Foster Homes of Relative Caregivers*, A-09-06-00023 (Oct. 2, 2009); and *Philadelphia County's Title IV-E Claims Based on Contractual Per Diem Rates of $300 or Less for Foster Care Services from October 1997 Through September 2002*, A-03-07-00560 (May 19, 2008).

[14] GAO, *Foster Care and Adoption Assistance: Federal Oversight Needed to Safeguard Funds and Ensure Consistent Support for States' Administrative Costs*, GAO-06-649 (Washington, D.C.: June 15, 2006).

[15] Examples of state-level audit reports include the following: California State Auditor, *State of California Internal Control and State and Federal Compliance Audit Report for the Fiscal Year Ended June 30, 2010* (Sacramento, Calif.: Mar. 29, 2011); KPMG, *Government of the District of Columbia Schedule of Expenditures of Federal Awards and Reports Required by Government Auditing Standards and OMB Circular A-133, Year Ended September 30, 2010* (Washington, D.C.: Jan. 27, 2011); and State of Indiana, State Board of Accounts, *State of Indiana Single Audit Report July 1, 2009 to June 30, 2010* (Indianapolis, Ind.: Feb. 25, 2011).

[16] In its fiscal year 2005 PAR, HHS reported an improper payment estimate for the Foster Care program for fiscal years 2004 and 2005. According to HHS, the fiscal year 2004 error rate had not been finalized prior to the issuance of its fiscal year 2004 PAR, and thus was not reported in that publication.

[17] In their fiscal year 2011 PARs and AFRs, select federal entities updated their fiscal year 2010 improper payment estimates to reflect changes since issuance of their fiscal year 2010 reports. These updates decreased the governmentwide improper payment estimate for fiscal year 2010 from $125.4 billion to $120.6 billion. Estimated improper payment amounts for fiscal years 2011 and 2010 may include estimates based on prior years' data, if current reporting year data were not available, as allowed by OMB guidance.

[18] The four programs with both the highest dollar estimates and highest error rates were the Earned Income Tax Credit, Unemployment Insurance, Medicare Advantage, and National School Lunch programs.

[19] GAO.

[20] The four risk-susceptible programs that did not report a required improper payments estimate for fiscal year 2011 were the Department of Education's Federal Family Education Loan, Federal Communications Commission's Interstate Telecommunications Relay Services Fund, and HHS's Children's Health Insurance Program and Temporary Assistance for Needy Families programs.

[21] The term state-administered refers to federal programs that are managed on a day-to-day basis at the state level to carry out program objectives.

[22] Pub. L. No. 111-3, 123 Stat. 8 (Feb. 4, 2009).

[23] DOD refers to payments to contractors and vendors collectively as commercial payments.

[24] GAO, *DOD Financial Management: Weaknesses in Controls over the Use of Public Funds and Related Improper Payments*, GAO-11-950T (Washington, D.C.: Sept. 22, 2011), and *Improper Payments: Significant Improvements Needed in DOD's Efforts to Address Improper Payment and Recovery Auditing Requirements*, GAO-09-442 (Washington, D.C.: July 29, 2009).

[25] DOD Inspector General, *DOD Needs to Improve High Dollar Overpayment Review and Reporting*, D-2011-050 (Arlington, Va.: Mar. 16, 2011).

[26] DOD Inspector General, *DOD Needs to Improve High Dollar Overpayment Review and Reporting*.

[27] DOD Inspector General, *DOD Needs to Improve High Dollar Overpayment Review and Reporting*. The IG report stated that DFAS and the Army Corps of Engineers did not review all payment systems for high-dollar overpayments. DFAS did not review approximately $2.2 billion in payments from five entitlement systems and the Corps of Engineers did not complete a timely review of $7.3 billion of commercial payments.

[28] GAO, *Improper Payments: Federal and State Coordination Needed to Report National Improper Payment Estimates on Federal Programs*, GAO-06-347 (Washington, D.C.:Apr. 14, 2006).

[29] GAO, *Improper Payments: Progress Made but Challenges Remain in Estimating and Reducing Improper Payments*, GAO-09-628T (Washington, D.C.: Apr. 22, 2009), and *Improper*

*Payments: Status of Agencies' Efforts to Address Improper Payment and Recovery Auditing Requirements*, GAO-08-438T (Washington, D.C.: Jan. 31, 2008).

[30] AFCARS is the federal information system that collects and processes data on children in foster care and those who have been adopted under the auspices of state child welfare agencies. AFCARS serves as the central depository of various nationwide data on the foster care program, as required by the Title IV-E legislation. ACF uses this system for, among other purposes, determining and assessing outcomes for children and families, budget planning and projections, and targeting areas for greater or potential technical assistance efforts. The data in AFCARS are self-reported and maintained by the states, and are subject to information system assessment reviews and federally mandated edit checks by ACF.

[31] The other types of errors identified related to eligibility. These included providers not licensed or approved, ineligible payments (e.g., therapy), a child not being eligible under the Aid to Families with Dependent Children program at the time of removal, criminal records check not completed, judicial determination regarding reasonable efforts to finalize permanency plan not timely, and no judicial determination of reasonable efforts to prevent removal.

[32] This analysis was based on the Title IV-E eligibility reviews that comprised the fiscal year 2010 Foster Care program improper payment estimate.

[33] GAO.

[34] "Pay and chase" refers to the labor-intensive and time-consuming practice of trying to recover overpayments once they have already been made rather than preventing improper payments in the first place.

[35] OMB Circular No. A-136 Revised, *Financial Reporting Requirements*, and OMB Memorandum M-10-13, *Issuance of Part III to OMB Circular A-123, Appendix C.*

[36] OMB defines these error types as: *Documentation and Administrative Errors* - Errors caused by the absence of supporting documentation necessary to verify the accuracy of a payment or errors caused by incorrect inputting, classifying, or processing of applications or payments by a relevant Federal agency, State agency, or third party who is not the beneficiary; *Authentication and Medical Necessity Errors* - Errors caused by an inability to authenticate eligibility criteria through third-party databases or other resources because no databases or other resources exist, or providing a service that was not medically necessary given the patient's condition; and *Verification Error*s - Errors caused by the failure or inability to verify recipient information, including earnings, income, assets, or work status, even though verifying information does exist in third-party databases or other resources (in this situation, as contrasted with "authentication" errors, the "inability" to verify may arise due to legal or other restrictions that effectively deny access to an existing database or resource), or errors due to beneficiaries failing to report correct information to an agency.

[37] 75 Fed. Reg. 35953 (June 23, 2010).

[38] The National Directory of New Hires database, maintained by HHS, contains information on all newly hired employees, quarterly wage reports for all employees, and unemployment insurance claims nationwide.

[39] Pub. L. No. 111-240, § 4241, 124 Stat. 2504, 2599 (Sept. 27, 2010).

[40] GAO, *Medicaid Program Integrity: Expanded Federal Role Presents Challenges to and Opportunities for Assisting States*, GAO-12-288T (Washington D.C.: Dec. 7, 2011).

[41] GAO, *Standards for Internal Control in the Federal Government*, GAO/AIMD-00-21.3.1 (Washington, D.C: November 1999).

[42] GAO, *Improper Payments: Reported Medicare Estimates and Key Remediation Strategies*, GAO-11-842T (Washington, D.C.: July 28, 2011).

[43] The One PI program portal is a web-based user interface that enables a single log-in through centralized, role-based access to the system.

[44] We reported in June 2011 that IDR includes most types of Medicare claims data, but not the Medicaid data needed to help analysts detect improper payments of Medicaid claims. See GAO, *Fraud Detection Systems: Centers for Medicare and Medicaid Services Needs to Ensure More Widespread Use*, GAO-11-475 (Washington D.C.: June 30, 2011).

[45] Pub. L. No. 109-432, div. B., title III, § 302, 120 Stat. 2922, 2991-92 (Dec. 20, 2006), *codified* at 42 U.S.C. § 1395ddd(h).

[46] Pub. L. No. 111-148, § 6411, 124 Stat. 119, 773 (Mar. 23, 2010).

[47] Pub. L. No. 103-354, § 281, 108 Stat. 3178, 3233 (Oct. 13, 1994), *codified, as amended, at* 7 U.S.C. § 7001.

[48] OMB's implementing guidance for IPERA allows agencies to use up to 25 percent of funds recovered under a payment recapture audit program for a financial management improvement program, including providing a portion of funding to state and local governments.

In: Improper Payments …
Editor: Jeffrey B. Powers

ISBN: 978-1-62948-844-8


*Chapter 3*

# TESTIMONY OF DANIEL I. WERFEL, CONTROLLER, OFFICE OF MANAGEMENT AND BUDGET. HEARING ON "CURBING FEDERAL AGENCY WASTE AND FRAUD: NEW STEPS TO STRENGTHEN THE INTEGRITY OF FEDERAL PAYMENTS"*

## INTRODUCTION

Thank you Chairman Carper, Ranking Member Coburn, and distinguished members of the Committee, for inviting me to discuss the Federal Government's efforts to prevent, reduce, and recapture improper payments. I appreciate the opportunity to provide an update on this important topic to the Committee, which has been at the forefront of moving us forward on addressing improper payments.

In practical terms, improper payments are payments made by the Government to the wrong entity, in the wrong amount, or for the wrong reason. Although not all improper payments are fraud, and not all improper payments represent a loss to the Government—since they include both

---

* This is an edited, reformatted and augmented version of a testimony, presented May 8, 2013 before the Senate Committee on Homeland Security and Governmental Affairs.

overpayments and underpayments—all improper payments degrade the integrity of Government programs.

This Administration has taken an aggressive approach to attacking waste, fraud, and abuse within Government agencies. Nowhere is this more apparent than in combatting improper payments. In FY 2009, the government-wide improper payment rate was at an all-time-high level of 5.42 percent. As a result of several actions taken by the Administration, the government-wide improper payment rate has steadily declined to 4.35 percent in FY 2012 (when Department of Defense commercial payments are factored in, the government-wide error rate falls to 3.7 percent). In addition, Federal agencies recaptured a record $4.4 billion in overpayments to contractors over the last three years, due in large part to the success of the Medicare Fee-for-Service Recovery Audit Contractor (RAC) program.

This is important progress, to be sure. However, I believe that there is much more work to be done, and that the amount of improper payments the government makes continues to be far too high.

## CURRENT AGENCY EFFORTS

The progress made to-date is largely driven by improper payment reductions in programs that typically have had high improper payment rates. In FY 2012, we saw improper payment rate reductions in a number of major Federal programs, including Medicare, Medicaid, Unemployment Insurance, the Earned Income Tax Credit, Supplemental Nutrition Assistance Program (Food Stamps), Pell Grants, the School Lunch program, and the Retirement, Survivors, and Disability Insurance. I would like to highlight some specific examples of what agencies are doing to reduce improper payments and improve program integrity.

### Health Care Fraud and Prevention

In an effort to reduce improper payments—including those that are fraud-related—the Department of Health and Human Services (HHS) is using new approaches to detect and prevent fraud at the Centers for Medicare & Medicaid Services (CMS). CMS launched the Fraud Prevention System (FPS) to analyze all Medicare Fee-for-Service claims using risk-based algorithms developed by CMS and the private sector, prior to payment, allowing CMS to take prompt action where appropriate. FPS detects suspicious claims and providers, which then allows CMS to target investigative resources appropriately and swiftly take administrative action when warranted.

To enhance the use of FPS, last year, CMS opened a new Command Center to identify fraud in Medicare and Medicaid more quickly and more effectively, and to stop the waste of Federal funds. The Command Center brings together Medicare and Medicaid officials, as well as law enforcement partners from the HHS Office of the Inspector General, the Federal Bureau of Investigation, and CMS's anti-fraud investigators. In addition, the Command Center gathers experts from all different areas—including clinicians, data analysts, fraud investigators, and policy experts—to build and improve state-of-the art predictive analytics that spot fraud quickly and effectively. As a result of this collaborative approach, the agency is able to more quickly initiate administrative actions, coordinate with law enforcement, and avert additional losses by holding potential fraud perpetrators accountable. The current approach to fighting health care fraud is paying off. For example, in FY 2012, fraud detection and enforcement efforts in the Health Care Fraud and Abuse Control (HCFAC) program resulted in the record-breaking recovery and return of $4.2 billion, a total that is double the program's annual historic average since 1997, and which resulted in an average return-oninvestment over the last three years of $7.90 for every $1.00 expended.

## Department of Defense Improper Payments

In FY 2012, the Department of Defense (DoD) estimated an improper payment rate for commercial payments at 0.02 percent. DoD plans to work on enhancing its sampling methodology to more fully consider the complexity of different types of payments for reporting in future years. Since 2008, DoD has been successful in identifying and preventing improper payments in its five largest commercial payment systems through use of the pre-payment Business Activity Monitoring (BAM) Program. The BAM Program uses data analytics and programming logic to identify and prevent erroneous payments to vendors, as well as payments for services not rendered. Root cause data captured during the transaction analysis is used to refine the analytic and programming framework to improve the detection capability. In FY 2012, this continuous refinement process resulted in the use of logic to detect when a payment is being made to the wrong entity. This new error detection has already resulted in the prevention of $108.3 million in payments to the wrong vendor.

## Tax Fraud and Tax Identity Theft

Tax refund fraud caused by identity theft is a serious problem that causes billions of dollars in revenue loss annually and has negative consequences not only for the Government but also for the innocent taxpayers directly affected. The Internal Revenue Service (IRS) has taken numerous steps to combat identity theft and protect taxpayers, and continually looks at ways to increase data security and protect taxpayers' identities thorough a specialized fraud unit. For the 2013 filing season, the IRS has expanded those efforts. For example, more than 3,000 IRS employees currently work on identity theft issues (more than double the number at the start of the previous filing season), and since the beginning of 2013, the IRS has worked with victims to resolve more than 200,000 cases of identity theft. In addition, IRS has intensified its fraud detection efforts by expanding the number and quality of its identity theft screening filters. Further, IRS suspended or rejected more than two million suspicious returns (including identity theft returns) so far this filing season. Other program integrity efforts at the Department of the Treasury are also leading to positive results in the Earned Income Tax Credit (EITC) program. In FY 2012, EITC reported an improper payment rate that was lower than in previous years.

## Department of Labor Improper Payments

The Department of Labor (DOL) has actively worked with the states to reduce improper payments in the Unemployment Insurance (UI) program. All states have been called to action to ensure that UI integrity is a top priority and to develop state specific strategies to bring down the overpayment rate. DOL also has provided states with supplemental funding to implement strategies and technology-based infrastructure investments that will help the states to prevent, detect, and recover UI overpayments. DOL's work with states in this area is beginning to prove successful, with the error rate declining from 12 percent in FY 2011 to 11.4 percent in FY 2012. Despite this success, we do see emerging challenges in this program that could potentially increase the improper payment rate, such as stricter state laws driving additional complexity on eligibility determinations.

To ensure that states actively own the responsibility of driving down the rate, DOL recently partnered with the New York Department of Labor to establish the UI Integrity Center of Excellence. New York has been a leader in combating improper payments in UI, and has made significant strides in recovering millions of dollars in fraudulent UI payments. This new Center will build upon these efforts and drive collaborative work with DOL and other states to develop and implement innovative integrity strategies that state UI programs can use to combat improper payments, and build capacity nationally to use data analytics and predictive modeling more effectively to support integrity efforts. The Center will leverage data analytics to identify the characteristics of claimants that commit fraud and create a methodology to act on those leads quickly to prevent, detect, and recover improper payments more effectively. Innovation also plays an important role in ensuring program integrity in the UI program. Under a pilot program funded by the Partnership Fund for Program Integrity Innovation, DOL has been working with the National Association of State Workforce Agencies (NASWA) and three partner states (Missouri, Illinois, and Mississippi), to test the value of matching financial transaction data against state unemployment insurance data to help states detect when a claimant may have returned to work and is no longer qualified for benefits. Results from a retrospective data match with states are still under review but are quite promising. They indicate that this new approach could enable states to detect potential overpayments much more quickly than existing matches allow, which could prevent tens of millions of dollars in improper payments every year if put into practice.

This is important progress made across a variety of programs. However, there is more work to be done. The Government still made nearly $108 billion in improper payments in 2012, which is an unacceptably high number and degrades the integrity of Government programs. Moreover, certain programs such as Medicare Advantage and the Rental Assistance program at the Department of Housing and Urban Development saw increases in their payment error rate, indicating that we have more to do to reduce error in these programs.

## Moving Forward

To help guide our future efforts, the Administration has set a new government-wide goal of reducing improper payments: by the end of FY 2016, we aim to achieve a minimum 97 percent government-wide accuracy rate, which translates to an improper payment rate of 3 percent or less. Today, I would like to highlight several important initiatives that will anchor our efforts in addressing improper payments and reaching our goal.

### The President's FY 2014 Budget

The President's FY 2014 Budget includes a suite of program integrity proposals that, if enacted, would result in an estimated $98 billion in total savings over 11 years. For example, the Budget proposes to establish a dependable source of mandatory funding for Continuing Disability Reviews (CDRs) and Supplemental Security Income (SSI) redeterminations, which would save an estimated $38 billion over 10 years. In addition, the Budget also continues to build upon a robust set of proposals to strengthen Medicare and Medicaid program integrity from last year's Budget and prior efforts.

There is compelling evidence that additional investments in program integrity can significantly decrease improper payments and recoup many times the initial outlay. For example, for every dollar spent by the Social Security Administration (SSA) on a disability review, the Government saves an estimated nine dollars in erroneous payments. In addition, historical rates of return for the Health Care Fraud and Abuse Control (HCFAC) program continue to grow. From 2010 to 2012, the program returned almost eight dollars for every dollar expended, as mentioned earlier in my testimony.

### Implementing the Do Not Pay Initiative

Under this Administration, the Federal Government has focused on leveraging technology and sharing data to address improper payments. In April 2012, the Administration launched the government-wide Do Not Pay effort to help agencies avoid making payments to individuals or entities who should not receive Federal funds, such as debarred contractors receiving Federal awards, or retirement benefits going to dead Federal employees. By providing a single point of access to an array of databases and using data analytics, we are equipping Federal agencies with new tools to stop improper payments before they occur.

Earlier this year, the President signed into law the Improper Payments Elimination and Recovery Improvement Act of 2012 (IPERIA), which will enhance the Administration's efforts to combat improper payments. Consistent with existing protections for individual data privacy, the new law will help improve the determination of improper payments by agencies, improve recovery of improper payments, and reinforce and accelerate the Administration's "Do Not Pay" efforts.

As required under IPERIA, agencies will begin checking all payments, as appropriate, through Do Not Pay by June 1, 2013. Over the past few months, the Office of Management and Budget and Treasury have worked to develop and enhance an initial working system that will allow for central screening of payments against Do Not Pay using payment information agencies previously provided to Treasury in the ordinary course of business. The first phase of Do Not Pay implementation will focus on matching recipients with public data from the Death Master File (DMF) and the System for Award Management (SAM, which includes the former Excluded Parties List). Treasury will provide reports to agencies, which will adjudicate hits and adjust pre-award and pre-payment procedures to ensure these procedures factor in relevant information from Treasury on potential disqualification from eligibility. This is only a first step, however, as there is much more to be done to ensure that Do Not Pay is the robust, comprehensive solution for ensuring payment eligibility that Congress and the President have envisioned. Access to additional, appropriate databases will be expanded as, among other things, each agency involved completes necessary data-sharing agreements and satisfies database-specific legal restrictions (including privacy safeguards).

To help bolster Do Not Pay's value and address other key Administration goals, the President's FY 2014 Budget includes two proposals related to improving access to, and the completeness of, death data. We estimate that the first proposal would prevent more than $1.3 billion in improper payments over 10 years by expanding Federal agency access to death data submitted by states for specific purposes that include program integrity. The second proposal would gradually phase in full implementation of electronic death records in all states and other vital records jurisdictions over four years, which would result in timelier and more accurate data in the Death Master File.

## CONCLUSION

I would like to close by emphasizing that this Administration will continue to treat improper payments as a key priority, and will continue to explore new and innovative ways to reduce, prevent, and recapture improper payments. I am proud of the progress we have made so far, but there is much work to be done to improve the accuracy and integrity of Federal payments. Therefore, I look forward to continuing to work with this Committee, as well as the Government Accountability Office and the Inspectors General community. All of these stakeholders are our partners in this endeavor, and they play a critical role in holding the Federal Government accountable for reducing improper payments.

Thank you again for inviting me to testify. I look forward to answering your questions.

# INDEX

## T



## U



## V



## W



## Y